Leadership and Small Business

Karise Hutchinson

Leadership and Small Business

The Power of Stories

Karise Hutchinson
University of Ulster
Coleraine, Londonderry, UK

ISBN 978-3-319-64776-0   ISBN 978-3-319-64777-7 (eBook)
DOI 10.1007/978-3-319-64777-7

Library of Congress Control Number: 2017948285

© The Editor(s) (if applicable) and The Author(s) 2018
This work is subject to copyright. All rights are solely and exclusively licensed by the Publisher, whether the whole or part of the material is concerned, specifically the rights of translation, reprinting, reuse of illustrations, recitation, broadcasting, reproduction on microfilms or in any other physical way, and transmission or information storage and retrieval, electronic adaptation, computer software, or by similar or dissimilar methodology now known or hereafter developed.
The use of general descriptive names, registered names, trademarks, service marks, etc. in this publication does not imply, even in the absence of a specific statement, that such names are exempt from the relevant protective laws and regulations and therefore free for general use.
The publisher, the authors and the editors are safe to assume that the advice and information in this book are believed to be true and accurate at the date of publication. Neither the publisher nor the authors or the editors give a warranty, express or implied, with respect to the material contained herein or for any errors or omissions that may have been made. The publisher remains neutral with regard to jurisdictional claims in published maps and institutional affiliations.

Cover illustration: Pattern adapted from an Indian cotton print produced in the 19th century

Printed on acid-free paper

This Palgrave Macmillan imprint is published by Springer Nature
The registered company is Springer International Publishing AG
The registered company address is: Gewerbestrasse 11, 6330 Cham, Switzerland

Like any journey, there is always a cost in reaching the final destination. The most significant cost was time, and as a finite resource the sacrifice was precious time with my family. So, to my husband and four children, Ali, Zachary, Finlay, Grace, and Samuel, I promise to make it up to you! There have been many others who have supported me in this journey contributing to the creation of this book. To my family and loyal friends, my champions, you know who you are, thank you.

While there are too many others to mention by name, I would like to especially thank my good friend and colleague Matthew Kearney. As my unofficial editor he generously and consistently gave me detailed feedback, but most of all encouraged me to keep the pace and complete the race. I am also deeply grateful to my official editor Madeleine Holder, who guided me in the journey, giving constructive feedback and answers to my many questions. In the search for metaphorical meaning in telling the story of small business, I would like to thank Hannah Reid for the lessons in plant biology.

I would particularly like to thank the entrepreneurial leaders who gave permission for me to invade their personal and professional space and craft their unique story of leading small business. It is a vulnerable endeavour that requires bravery, but I know the integrity and honesty that inspired me will inspire many others who read this book. There is one storyteller's support and encouragement that deserves special dedication—to Jayne Taggart who believed in my idea and was prepared to invest time and finance to make it happen, thank you.

Foreword

When Karise Hutchinson asked me to write the foreword to her book, I was delighted. Frankly, I can think of no more important or potentially profitable ventures for people embarking on a career in leadership than rediscovering their purpose and developing their Authentic Leadership. Over the past decade, I have worked with thousands of executives, most from large or multinational firms, helping them reclaim their leadership purpose and align it with the organizations in which they lead. In a world that changes every day, in which strategic plans are obsolete before the budget cycle runs its course, these leaders confirm again and again that having clarity of purpose is the only way to steer towards success.

The many benefits of clarity of purpose show up in both our personal and professional lives. This is perhaps never truer than in a small company, where the leader's purpose is inextricably identified with the organization's. After all, over the course of building a career or a business, purpose is probably the only thing that will hold true and remain constant.

Now Karise Hutchinson brings the power of Authentic Leadership and leadership purpose to the world of small business—the fastest growing sector in the world economy, responsible for almost half of private sector employment in the USA and the UK. Small business owners, even if they have just a few employees, are first and foremost leaders. Harvard Business Review research has shown that employees of purpose-led organizations are much more engaged, satisfied, and like to stay and continue to contribute to the organization. The effect was further magnified when the employees felt that their leader was clear about his or her purpose and communicated it to them. This book, with its focus on story-telling as a way to discover, reclaim, and communicate personal and organizational purpose, holds the key to that.

When I first met Karise in one of our Leadership Purpose programs, we discovered her own purpose statement, "Realise and mobilise excellence in a beautiful way that brings life and light." *Leadership and Small Business: the Power of Stories* is a perfect expression of that purpose, as it offers readers a way to mobilize excellence and bring light in their own lives. As Karise reminds us, all big businesses were once small. By attending to the lessons in this book, many readers will find the pathway to growth.

Nick Craig
President of Authentic Leadership Institute
Harvard, USA

Preface

The once upon a time of this book begins some years ago when I embarked on my doctoral research at Ulster University. The study of small business from that early point has guided my research enthusiasm ever since. I have always taken an applied approach to my research, exploring the theoretical perspectives as well as industry impact. Indeed, there is also no doubt married to a small business owner for over 21 years has also grounded my research in the reality of doing business! The curiosity in researching leadership derives from both my own story of learning to lead as a young Head of Department in a large Business School some years ago. It was also my commitment to helping others develop their leadership capacity whether student, business owner, or school teacher in Uganda (where I worked with Fields of Life and 50 school teachers) that forged this new mandate around leadership purpose in the field of small business.

As a student, I remember my fascination with the stories told by my lecturers that brought various subject matters to life. So, I was always keen to make sure I was the storyteller in addition to educator in the classroom. While the book reflects much of what I have learned from doing leadership, most of all it is evidenced by my experience of working with over 50 entrepreneurial leaders in the Lead2Grow programme, recognised by the British Academy of Management Education Practice award in 2016. As a social scientist, I believe the business leader's life story exists as a powerful resource not only for leadership itself and the study therein, but as role model for other businesses. The storytelling by entrepreneurial leaders in real time demonstrates the power of stories as well as the significance of leading with purpose. To this end, the book is written for student's studying small business management and or leadership, as well as small business leaders and practitioners seeking to find purpose in achieving their professional and personal goals.

Depending on the interests of reader, there are several ways to read this book instead of reading chapters in sequence. If primarily interested in the stories from entrepreneurial small business leaders, the reader can go to the introduction where the scene is set followed by Chaps. 7 and 8. Or, if the reader is a practitioner in the area of leadership development and would like to explore ideas for small business programmes, then it is recommended to read Chaps. 4 and 5, followed by the learning to lead in Chap. 6. However, if the reader is a student or anyone who is keen to understand the whole narrative from beginning to end, then it is most beneficial to read the book and all chapters in its entirety to grasp a full understanding of the story of leading small business.

Coleraine, UK   Karise Hutchinson

Contents

1	**Introduction**	1
1.1	Setting the Scene	2
1.2	Purpose and Scope of the Book	3
1.3	Research for the Book	4
1.4	Preview of Chapters	5
	1.4.1 Chapter 2 the Story of Small Business	5
	1.4.2 Chapter 3 Leadership in Small Firms—The X Factor	5
	1.4.3 Chapter 4 Leadership Purpose	6
	1.4.4 Chapter 5 Stories and Storytelling for Small Business Leaders	6
	1.4.5 Chapter 6 Learning to Lead: A New Model	6
	1.4.6 Chapter 7 Storytelling: Starting Out	7
	1.4.7 Chapter 8 Storytelling: 10 Years on	7
	1.4.8 Chapter 9 Conclusion	7
1.5	Chapter Summary	8
References		8

Contents

2	**The Story of Small Business**	**11**
2.1	Introduction- Use of Metaphors	12
	2.1.1 Metaphorical Expressions in Business and Management	13
	2.1.2 Metaphor of Plant Botany for Small Business	14
2.2	Unique Contribution	16
2.3	Defining Characteristics of Small Business Species	17
	2.3.1 Definition	18
	2.3.2 Characteristics	18
	2.3.3 Variety	20
2.4	Development and Growth	21
	2.4.1 Life Cycle	21
	2.4.2 Ecosystem	23
	2.4.3 Market Exchange	25
2.5	Chapter Summary	27
	References	27
3	**Leadership in Small Firms—The X Factor**	**31**
3.1	Introduction	32
3.2	Study of Leadership in Small Business Management	33
3.3	Entrepreneurial Leadership	35
	3.3.1 Theoretical Intersection	36
	3.3.2 Characteristics of Entrepreneurial Leaders	37
3.4	Leadership Impact and Intervention	38
	3.4.1 Economic Productivity and Ambition Debate	39
	3.4.2 Business Impact	40
	3.4.3 Barriers to Leadership Training and Development	42
	3.4.4 Interventions in the Ecosystem	44
3.5	Chapter Summary	47
	References	48
4	**Leadership Purpose**	**53**
4.1	Introduction	53
4.2	Authentic Leadership	54
	4.2.1 Growing Interest	54
	4.2.2 Defining Authentic Leadership	55

		4.2.3	Clarifying Authentic Leadership	56
		4.2.4	The Debate	57
	4.3	Leading with Purpose		58
		4.3.1	Roots of Purpose	58
		4.3.2	The 'What' and 'Why' of Leadership Purpose	58
		4.3.3	Integration of Purpose	60
	4.4	Significance for Small Business		62
		4.4.1	Purpose and Profits	63
		4.4.2	Purpose and People	63
		4.4.3	Mobilising Purpose	64
	4.5	Chapter Summary		66
	References			66
5	**Stories and Storytelling for Small Business Leaders**			**69**
	5.1	Growing Importance		70
		5.1.1	Once upon a Time….	70
		5.1.2	Art or Science?	71
		5.1.3	Changing Narrative	71
	5.2	Business Context		72
		5.2.1	Multidisciplinary Validation	72
		5.2.2	Metaphor as Story	73
		5.2.3	Business Case	74
	5.3	Leadership Purpose		75
		5.3.1	The 'Story' of Leadership Purpose	75
		5.3.2	Finding the Story	76
		5.3.3	Defining the Story	79
		5.3.4	Telling the Story	81
	5.4	Chapter Summary		84
	References			84
6	**Learning to Lead: A New Model**			**89**
	6.1	Introduction		90
	6.2	Leadership Development in Small Firms		90
		6.2.1	Action Learning for Small Firm Leaders	92
	6.3	Exploring a Solution for Micro Firms		93
		6.3.1	Gap Analysis	94
		6.3.2	Designing the Solution	94

		6.3.3	Learning from Harvard	100
	6.4	Pedagogic Review		101
	6.5	Lead2grow Model		103
		6.5.1	Business and Leader Impact	105
		6.5.2	Regional Economic Impact	106
	6.6	Summary Chapter		107
References				107
7	**Storytelling: Starting Out**			**111**
	7.1	Introduction		112
	7.2	Karen Yates: Taylor Yates		112
		7.2.1	Finding a Purpose	113
		7.2.2	Role Models and Game Changers	114
		7.2.3	Recessionary Learning	115
		7.2.4	Leading at the Starting Line	116
	7.3	Ricky Martin: Skunkworks Surf Co		117
		7.3.1	'Blood Brother' Leadership	118
		7.3.2	Leading from Idea to Reality	119
		7.3.3	Growing the Family	121
		7.3.4	Award Winning Leadership	122
	7.4	Danielle Tagg: Articlave Day Nursery		123
		7.4.1	Pioneering a New Adventure	124
		7.4.2	Developing My Team	125
		7.4.3	Rewards of Learning	126
	7.5	Aaron Mcconnell: Vynomic		128
		7.5.1	In the Beginning	128
		7.5.2	Learning to Pivot the Business	130
		7.5.3	Building a Boat	132
		7.5.4	Leading on Purpose	133
	7.6	Chapter Summary		134
8	**Storytelling: 10 Years On**			**135**
	8.1	Introduction		136
	8.2	Jayne Taggart: Causeway Enterprise Agency		136
		8.2.1	Master Gardener	137
		8.2.2	Gardening in a Crisis	138

		8.2.3	Survival Seeds	140
	8.3	John Armstrong: Armstrong Medical	142
		8.3.1	Creating Support for Life	143
		8.3.2	The Illusion of Paradise	144
		8.3.3	Refiners Fire	145
		8.3.4	Changing Gear	146
	8.4	Mark Mckinney: ATG Group	148
		8.4.1	Dream and a Prayer	149
		8.4.2	In the 'Fishing' Business	150
		8.4.3	Giving a Second Chance	151
		8.4.4	'We Are Going to Need a Bigger Boat….' (Jaws, 1975)	152
	8.5	Karen Gardiner: Ground Espresso Bars	154
		8.5.1	Challenge-Driven	155
		8.5.2	Building a Fleet	156
		8.5.3	Charting New Waters	157
		8.5.4	Drinking an Ethical Cup of Coffee	158
	8.6	Chapter Summary	160
9	**Conclusion**	163
	9.1	Plot of Story	163
	9.2	Main Character—The Small Business Leader	165
	9.3	A Happy Ending?	166
	References	168
Index				171

List of Figures

Fig. 2.1	Small business life cycle path	22
Fig. 5.1	The 'story' of leadership purpose	76
Fig. 6.1	Phase one Lead2Grow programme	97
Fig. 6.2	Phase two Lead2Grow programme	99
Fig. 6.3	Lead2Grow model	104
Fig. 9.1	Plot of the story—converging ideas	164

List of Images

Image 7.1	Karen Yates	113
Image 7.2	Ricky and Chris Martin	118
Image 7.3	Danielle Tagg	124
Image 7.4	Aaron McConnell	129
Image 8.1	Jayne Taggart	142
Image 8.2	John Armstrong	148
Image 8.3	Mark McKinney	154
Image 8.4	Karen Gardiner	160

List of Tables

Table 2.1	Plant-small business dictionary	15
Table 3.1	Entrepreneurial leadership as a new paradigm	37

1

Introduction

Abstract The setting of this book is the small business organisation where the leader takes center stage. Small business leaders are all too often unsung heroes in spite of employing nearly half of the UK's private sector workforce. They are worthy of attention not just due to population size and density, but because they provide the success stories of the future. After all, big businesses were once upon small. To this end, the purpose of this book is to tell their story of leading business, bringing together theoretical and practical perspectives. In outlining the narrative, the first chapter provides the rationale for leading with purpose in a small business context, as well as the practice of storytelling in leadership learning and development. The final sections therein provide a preview of the chapters to come.

Keywords Small business · Leadership · Stories · Storytelling · Purpose Authentic leadership · Lead2Grow · Entrepreneurial leaders · Research Chapter previews

1.1 Setting the Scene

Leadership is arguably one of the most discussed and debated academic subjects, and no more so than in the field of business. But, new challenges in the world of business are bringing new and serious levels of confusion and stress to the leaders of organisations. In a time of extraordinary uncertainty and exceptional turbulence, business organisations require all of the leader's capacity, as well as shared responsibility by the whole team in order to survive. Yet, amid the plethora of leadership books, research articles, documentaries, and media, it is evident today people respond differently to leadership than they used to. Not only must leaders bounce back rapidly from catastrophic events and display resilience, but they also must find meaning and connection in relationships. In this new wave of leadership there is a greater focus on the follower, who seeks a different culture of leadership found in authentic or genuine leaders who know their purpose and work with courage.

The demands are the same for leaders of big or small businesses. However, the spotlight on large organisations over the years has failed to account for the distinct leadership challenges and opportunities of leading a small business. In countries across the globe, small businesses make the significant majority of the business populations. They are all too often unsung heroes in spite of employing nearly half of the UK's private sector workforce. Government and professional body organisations have published various reports on leadership capability in small firms as a key function of survival and growth with significant impact upon economic productivity. Yet, within academia there is little recognition of the leadership concept in a small business context. Characterised by one-person centred organisational structure and highly personal approach to management, these business owners are intrinsically different in their approach to leading, solving business problems and making decisions. Not only deserving of attention from theoretical, practical and policy perspectives, we do well to remember it is small businesses that often provide the success stories of the future; after all big businesses were once upon small.

1.2 Purpose and Scope of the Book

The overall aim of the book is to provoke interest in, and generate new knowledge of, small business leadership. Specifically, it seeks to first, help the reader understand why purpose driven leadership is critical in business terms and especially for small firms. For small business owners this can present a significant challenge; the practice and concept of leadership is often considered irrelevant even though they are "doing" leadership everyday (Barnes et al. 2015). Secondly, to explain how stories help find leadership purpose for the small business owner, and finally, to explore how storytelling communicates purpose effectively to others in a way that yields real business impact. There are many texts about the small business organisation, but none that bring to life the story of small business leaders and their personal and professional development. Demonstrating the power of storytelling that can reach minds and touch hearts (Forman 2013), this book captures the narrative of leading with purpose in real time by focusing on the stories told by small business leaders at different stages in the journey (see Chaps. 7, 8).

According to Harvard research, purpose is touted as the key to navigating the complex volatile and ambiguous world today, where strategy is ever-changing and few decisions are obviously right or wrong (Craig and Snooks 2014). So, taking on board the relevance of authentic leadership theory and building upon the Harvard model of purpose driven leadership, this book explores the application of this ethos in a way that connects the purpose of the owner manager to the growth and performance of the business. From this, a new model of leadership development for very small firms is proposed built from the author's recent empirical research and experience of working with entrepreneurs in the small business sector, underpinned by the ethos of purpose driven leadership. Unlike the approach of traditional case studies told with the benefit of hindsight and written to illustrate a point, the metaphorical expression and storytelling herein invites participation by the reader, whether lecturer, student, practitioner or small business entrepreneur in the story of small business leadership.

1.3 Research for the Book

My research for this book derives from a range of sources and experiences. With a Ph.D. in small business management, the focus of attention has always been the small firm, encompassing the dimensions of internationalisation, marketing, management, and business support. More recently, lecturing in the area of leadership and management teaching undergraduate and postgraduate students on the subject have provided a sound knowledge of the theoretical perspectives of this vast subject. Perhaps most important, over the course of the last four years has been experience of designing and delivering different small business leadership programmes. The Lead2Grow model draws upon primary research with over 50 entrepreneurial leaders of micro firms registered on two leadership development programmes.

In search for a relevant theoretical perspective for understanding small business leadership and development, it was taking part in a leadership programme by the Authentic leadership Institute based in Harvard that was the starting point of a new journey. This experience brought to life the benefits of leadership purpose, and provided the underpinning ethos for the development of small business leaders applied in the Lead2Grow programmes of learning designed and delivered by the author. Some of the entrepreneurial leaders in Chaps. 7 and 8 took part in the learning and other did not, but regardless, each story illustrates the significance of knowing and driving purpose with real business benefits. In crafting each story, the author worked closely with the entrepreneur, but the data was also triangulated with various secondary sources to ensure validity. Telling your story is not an easy task, identified in the literature as a challenge for many leaders (Guber 2007). Ultimately, it proved that despite the vulnerability and self-awareness required in the process, the opportunity to make a bigger difference by inspiring and informing was reward enough.

1.4 Preview of Chapters

1.4.1 Chapter 2 the Story of Small Business

Chapter 2 presents the 'why' of small business underlining their significance from theoretical, practitioner, and policy perspectives. The discussion seeks to capture the key aspects of small business that provides an understanding for the subsequent discussion of leadership, without rewriting existing textbook and research publications. Applying the art of storytelling, the world of plant life is used as a metaphor to capture the distinctiveness of small businesses and their operations as well as providing better understanding of their significant social and economic contribution.

1.4.2 Chapter 3 Leadership in Small Firms—The X Factor

The owner of the small firm plays centre stage in the story of the small business organisation and warrants the focus of attention in the third chapter. Discussion herein seeks to rectify low recognition of the small business leadership phenomenon and the weak desire to study it (Kempster 2009). In doing so, it provides a much needed and detailed examination of leadership as the X factor of small business survival and success (CMI 2015). While large businesses may be able to survive for short periods without great leadership, the opposite is true for small businesses. Comprised of few employees and some without any, the small business quickly falls apart without strong leadership purpose and capability. Understanding that leadership in larger and more established organisations cannot be transposed into the small business context, the theoretical discussion focuses on entrepreneurial leadership theory and the role of specific intervention measures for the sector.

1.4.3 Chapter 4 Leadership Purpose

In the saturated space of leadership theories, Chap. 4 focuses on the growing interest and relevance of the leadership purpose ethos for small business. Although the notion of 'purpose' is not a new one, academic research into leadership purpose for small business is scarce and almost always told from the perspective of large multinational corporations. Acknowledging the roots of leadership purpose in authentic leadership theory, the chapter presents the correlation between purpose and action by drawing upon the work of Craig and Snooks (2014). Specifically, the chapter points out the practical relevance and benefits of leadership purpose for small firms and how it can address market failure enabling leaders to improve performance and grow the organisation.

1.4.4 Chapter 5 Stories and Storytelling for Small Business Leaders

Chapter 5 unpacks the sense-making capability of stories and storytelling in the context of leading small business. Focusing on the growing importance of stories, the discussion provides justification of application in the world of business, where it has traditionally has found a more lukewarm reception. The chapter explains the science and art of storytelling, forming the argument that a story can build a narrative for topics that go deeper and live longer in a person's psyche than other forms of communication (Forman 2013). Building on the leadership purpose ethos, a new model underpinned by the power of stories and storytelling is presented with three key stages discussed in more detail in this chapter.

1.4.5 Chapter 6 Learning to Lead: A New Model

Following previous discussions, Chap. 6 focuses on the distinct learning requirements for small business leaders. Notwithstanding the challenges in making time for new learning, it is well known small business leaders must have the willingness to learn and apply that learning across the organisation if they want to succeed and grow. Interweaving theoretical discussions on leadership development and learning in small firms with new empirical research by the author focused on micro firms, this chapter presents the Lead2Grow model. The distinctiveness of the model encompasses critical areas of practice for micro firm leaders, defined by Lord Young as the vital 95% of businesses in the UK.

1.4.6 Chapter 7 Storytelling: Starting Out

Understanding the high failure rate of small businesses in the first five years, this chapter tells the story of entrepreneurial small business leadership early in their formation. Four remarkable entrepreneurial leaders tell their story in the moment of leading their business. Regardless of industry sector, the stories in this chapter reveal a golden thread personified in the leader's self-awareness, resilience and ambition in that they know their purpose and are growing their business against the odds.

1.4.7 Chapter 8 Storytelling: 10 Years on

The stories from entrepreneurial leaders who have successfully navigated the challenges of business for more than ten years provide critical insight into the longer journey of leadership as well as the lessons learned along the way. This chapter presents a diverse portfolio of stories told by business leaders operating in a wide range of sectors from environmental waste solutions to coffee, medical production to business support services.

1.4.8 Chapter 9 Conclusion

Chapter 9 of the book will present a summary of the synopsis of the plot and the main character in the story of leading small business. This includes the key issues and debate across all aspects of the book as well as a summary of the lessons learned in the form of five home truths. With a final call to action, the chapter will outline a number of key recommendations for future work and study in small business leadership.

1.5 Chapter Summary

The context of this book is the small business organisation, but the focus of analysis is the leader. It tells the story of leadership purpose that yields real business impact for the small firm underpinned by a strong emphasis on learning and development over time. We can easily read about the global success of entrepreneurs such as Richard Branson and Steve Jobs, but less is known about what it is really like once upon a time. The benefit of hindsight brings rose tinted spectacles, so the perspective of this book is leadership in the moment and told by small business owners in real time at various stages in the journey. In many ways the whole story is not new, just untold and deserving of attention in this book.

References

Barnes, S., S. Kempster, and S. Smith. 2015. *Leading small business: Business growth through leadership development*. Cheltenham, GL: Edward Elgar Publishing.
CMI (Chartered Management Institute). 2015. Growing your small business: The role of business schools and professional bodies. *Chartered Management Institute Publication*, September.
Craig, N., and S. Snooks. 2014. From purpose to impact: Figure out your passion and put it to work. *Harvard Business Review* 92 (5): 105–111.

Forman, J. 2013. *Storytelling in business: The authentic and fluent organisation*. Stanford, CA: Stanford Business Books.

Guber, P. 2007. The four truths of the storyteller. *Harvard Business Review* 85 (12): 52–59.

Kempster, S. 2009. Observing the invisible: Examining the role of observational learning in the development of leadership practice. *Journal of Management Development* 28 (5): 439–456.

2

The Story of Small Business

Abstract This chapter presents the 'why' of small business underlining their importance from theoretical, practitioner, and policy perspectives. Avoiding repetition of existing textbooks and research articles on the subject and demonstrating the art of storytelling, Hutchinson uses the world of plant life as a metaphor to better understand the small business organisation. The narrative is developed through a number of relevant metaphorical expressions that capture the distinctiveness of small businesses and their operations as well as providing better understanding of their significant social and economic contribution.

Keywords Small business · Leadership · Stories · Metaphorical expression · Plants · Entrepreneur · Small business owner · Leader Characteristics · Definition · Growth · Ecosystem

2.1 Introduction- Use of Metaphors

Since the work of Penrose in 1959 and some years later the Bolton Report (1971) published by the Committee of Inquiry on Small Firms, there has been meaningful and detailed attention paid to the small business enterprise from academic, practitioner and policy perspectives. This chapter seeks to capture the key aspects of small business to provide a foundation of understanding for the subsequent exploration and discussion of leadership, without rewriting existing textbook and research publications. To demonstrate the richness of the phenomenon beyond quantifiable aspects, the story of small business is told by the use of metaphorical expression. But, before telling the story, there is merit in first explaining why this tool is appropriate in the context of this book. People think in metaphors. Among cognitive scientists, there is a strong theory of the role of metaphor:

> Our ordinary conceptual system, interims of which we both think and act, is fundamentally metaphorical in nature. (Lakoff and Johnson 1980: 1)

In the field of cognitive linguistics, it is claimed people become familiar with new concepts via metaphorical thinking (Lakoff and Johnson 1980; Gentner and Jeziorski 1993). People learn in metaphors. According to Skorczynska (2014), metaphor has been used for many years to successfully facilitate education, fulfilling a number of functions such as creating new perspectives, enabling categorisation or aiding memorisation. As White (2003) explains, metaphors can be used as sense-making, abstract reasoning tools, and in his experience, for the purposes of teaching formal economics to students of a non-English speaking origin. Metaphors are multimodal encompassing other communication beyond written form to include sound, static and moving images, music, non-verbal sound and gestures (Skorczynska 2014). The multidimensional aspect of the metaphor is very much evident in the practice of business, often used to strengthen the marketing and strategy of the organisation (Friedman 2016) in various communication activities from oral presentations to negotiations and branding projects. Notwithstanding the impact of using a metaphor, the juxtaposition is not a perfect match to reality (Cardon et al. 2005), but rather more reflective of abstract thinking. Unlike literal truths, they require reflection, unpacking. For both of these reasons, they are likely to prove a useful addition to our didactic armory, facilitating students' grasp of what it feels like to be an entrepreneur (Cardon et al. 2005).

2.1.1 Metaphorical Expressions in Business and Management

Across the field of business management in subjects like economics, business organisation, strategy and entrepreneurship a range of metaphorical expression is found. For instance, broadly speaking most metaphors in business strategy relates to sport for example, 'doing business is like playing a game', or war for example 'fighting the competition'. Whereas, the specific use of biological metaphors in business and economics to explain largely abstract concepts reaches back seven decades when economists used Darwinian logic to explain the profit maximisation focus of the field by noting that firms that did not maximise profit would eventually fail (Marshall 1925). Other metaphors such as the economy as a plant, animal, human or machine have also been applied in the context of economics (White 2003). In a similar way to the plant metaphor which both share the nature of living organism, the animal and human metaphorical sources are used to describe growth collocations for instance 'green shoots of recovery', 'bloated economy', 'the aggressive growth of the tiger countries' (White 2003).

In the study of entrepreneurship, some related metaphors are used repeatedly, such as biological metaphors in organisational ecology. While not used by management scholars, relational metaphors have been applied to the concept of entrepreneurship to highlight the importance of emotions in entrepreneurial processes (Cardon et al. 2005). This study proposes that parenting, with its nurturance, passion, or even neglect or abuse, offers a particularly fruitful metaphor for examining entrepreneurship that may better resonate with entrepreneurs than current theory (Cardon et al. 2005). By examining the stages in the entrepreneurial and human procreation processes, comparing the founding of a new firm to the birth of a child, they seek to make entrepreneurship less heroic and more congruent with everyday experience, by grounding it in an experience that most human beings have had—as a parent, as a child, or both. In particular, the use of parenting metaphor highlights the importance of passion (i.e., strong emotions and enthusiasm) and identification (i.e., close association and connection) between an entrepreneur and a venture. Research in this area also proposes the life narratives of entrepreneurs as a research methodology (Aldrich 1992) that gives meaning to their stories of life and business (explained later in Chap. 5).

2.1.2 Metaphor of Plant Botany for Small Business

Aligned to mainstream cognitive linguistics theory and research by White (2003) that demonstrates the preference for more conventional forms of metaphor as opposed to more abstract and creative descriptions, the subsequent discussion will utilise the metaphor of plant life to present the story of small businesses. In doing so, provide better understanding of their key aspects as well significant social and economic contribution. This is justified in two ways. Firstly, the growth of plants as a metaphor for our times is not too abstract for understanding business today (Harberd 2007). The salient feature of a plant is the propensity for growth and the fact this growth may vary widely under different circumstances either in external and internal environment. This includes reference to the cyclic situation of growth whereby positive factors would contribute to growth and negative factors would on other hand impede growth (White 2003). Take for instance the economic impact of Brexit with significant repercussions for all businesses, regardless of specific sector, large or small.

Secondly, there are powerful principles embodied in the design and structure of a plant as it relates to business (Krogue 2012), as well as the

Table 2.1 Plant-small business dictionary

Metaphorical expression	Small business application
Plant as living organism	Small business entity
Species	Type of small business
Stem /leaves /flowers	Internal resources of the firm
Roots	Owner/founder of the business
Photosynthesis	Marketing exchange
Plant community	Variety of small business e.g. sole trader, family owned
Ecosystem	Interaction of business support, policy intervention, owner networks with business

Source Authors own

plant ecosystem. For instance, there are three principle organs- roots, stems and leaves make up the structure of the typical plant. The roots are akin to the owner/founder of the business in that they act as an anchor and affect the adaptation of the plant. Plants produce their own food by a chemical process called photosynthesis, using water, carbon dioxide and the energy of sunlight, which are essential to survive and thrive. In the same way businesses need cash flow, expertise and knowledge to exist, but given the resource constraints inherent with small businesses, this can be problematic.

To aid subsequent discussion, Table 2.1 presents a dictionary of terms and expressions of the plant metaphor, which will be explained throughout the remaining chapter. With no expertise in botany, but as a social scientist, the plant metaphor is thus explained in high-level terms without the complexity of terminology and equations, and is therefore not a pure reflection of scientific fact (approach justified by Cardon et al. 2005).

Subsequent discussion in this chapter will utilise the world of plant life as the basic source for the conceptualisation of small business, with core growth vocabulary. This metaphor is realised and expanded through a number of relevant illustrative expressions to capture the meaning of small business, structure, functions, as well as external and internal environmental influences. Application of the plant metaphor helps to give meaning to the narrative of small business, which is most often told in more quantifiable manner in textbooks, research articles, and industry articles, as well as in the classroom.

2.2 Unique Contribution

Plants are essential to the balance of nature and in people's lives. As photosynthesisers, they provide organic molecules for the food for the entire ecosystem, producing oxygen required by almost all living organisms. In a similar way, small businesses are recognised as the fabric of community, as well as the backbone of the economy. In everyday life, we rely on small businesses. Whether it's the daily visit to the local coffee shop, the parts manufacturer that employs a member of your family, the boutique retail shop where you find the unique gift for a friend, or the accountancy firm that helps you manage your finances, small businesses help to shape local towns and regions (Longworth 2014). Therefore, their significance is evident both in terms of serving local needs as well as serving the requirements of big businesses and public sector organisations. Take for instance, the role of small, independent food retailers, which are especially important to elderly, low-income, or limited mobility consumers (Wrigley 2002) who depend on these local stores to provide fresh, high quality ingredients and products. This particular type of small business has a social role in preventing food poverty and social exclusion in local communities (Cummins and Macintyre 2002; Broadbridge and Parsons 2003).

The small business sector in the UK has come far, leaping from 'doomed to extinction' in the 1960s and 1970s to 'backbone of the economy' as described recently by Prime Minister Teresa May and others. The Federation of Small Business (FSB 2016) argues that the productivity of the UK is dependent in part on the survival and growth of small businesses. Likewise, in the US, a large component of the economy relies on the success of small business (Valdiserri and Wilson 2010). According to Fuller (2001) small businesses in the US are engines of economic growth through employment and innovation. As Storey (1994) and others (e.g. Bridge and O'Neill 2013) point out a number of reasons for the revival of the small businesses. In economic terms, supply factors include technological changes (new products and industries), cost advantages (sub contracting), unemployment (redundancy and education), and policy (privatisation, deregulation and tax benefits). Demand factors on other hand include: structural changes (demand for services and variety), uncertainty of demand (individual customer requirements), macro economic conditions (unemployment) and economic developments (services, just in time and niches), as presented by Bridge and O'Neill (2013).

Not just in the UK, but the contribution small firms in general make to the economy of any country is increasing and their importance is now widely recognised (Barnes et al. 2015). Indeed, they often provide the success stories of the future; after all big businesses were once upon small. According to the Federation of Small Business, small businesses account for 48% of private-sector employment in the UK and there has been sustained growth in the small business population since the year 2000. But, the majority of this population growth has been the due to sole trader organisation. Indeed, two thirds of small businesses are owned and run by one person with no additional employees. Taking this into account, the significance of small business is inextricably linked to entrepreneurship, which has been recognised by government as a vital contributor to the health of the economy and the diversity of opportunity in society. As a result and since the 1980s, there has been an explosion of research into entrepreneurship and the small firm (Bridge and O'Neill 2013).

2.3 Defining Characteristics of Small Business Species

In the Kingdom of Plantae, species are living organisms that range in size and are photosynthetic, eukaryotic, and multicellular in feature belonging to various plant communities. Understanding the unique features of plants as well as how to define the species, constitutes similar deliberation in the small business literature. Some contend small businesses cannot be studied until they are defined, yet in reality others argue they must be studied before they can be defined (Bridge and O'Neill 2013). Regardless of the order of priority, the subsequent discussion will provide an overview of the areas incorporating the definition, characteristics, and variety of small businesses.

2.3.1 Definition

Botanists define plants according to vascular (producing seeds) and nonvascular (producing no seeds) and within these categories each type of plant species performs a specific niche role in the ecosystem. In defining small business organisations, size is typically assessed by the number of employees, outlets, annual turnover, or a combination of measures. There are a wide range of official classifications of small business by various organisations including definitions by Companies Act, Corporation Tax, British Bankers' Association and the US Small Business Administration, demonstrating how different definitions exist for different purposes. A quantifiable explanation is provided the EU Commission (2009), which defines the SME (small to medium-sized enterprise) according to employees, turnover, and total balance sheet.

Notwithstanding the plethora of definitions, there is no standard agreement on what constitutes a small business. Some argue that the quantifiable definitions of small firms serve as a proxy for what the essence of 'smallness' in business units, whereas people 'feel' they know what it is meant by a small business (Bridge and O'Neill 2013). Therefore, it can be more appropriate to define a company in the context of its absolute and relative size in the market place in which it operates (Paliwoda and Thomas 1998) and the influence it might have on that industry. For example, in relation to other businesses in the same sector, a ten person window cleaning business would be very large whereas 100 employee car manufacturer would be classified as very small (Bridge and O'Neill 2013). While there is a lack of universal agreement on how small firms are defined, there is more consensus in the literature as to their key characteristics (McAuley 2001), which is discussed in the next section.

2.3.2 Characteristics

Botanists explain plant anatomy as consisting of three main organs including the roots, stem, and leaf, as well as reproductive structures such as flowers or fruits. Plants exhibit natural variation in their form and structure expressed in many different forms. In a similar way this reflects the small business as an organisation. The root of a plant (which serves as an anchor to absorb water and minerals for use, storage and conduction) may be likened to the owner/founder who determines the direction and character of the small business. The stem function is to support the growth of the plant, while leaves of the plant allow photosynthesis to occur, signifying the importance of leveraging resources for small business owners to develop and grow. There are key characteristics that make small business entities distinct from larger organisations.

Some time ago, the Bolton Report (1971), described small firms as having a small share of the market; managed in a personalised way by its owners or part owners and does not have an elaborate management structure. Moreover, typical differences between small and large firms are defined by Davis et al. (1985):

- Small firms typically develop and implement strategies within severe resource constraints;
- Small firms typically lack specialised expertise and often have difficulty in purchasing this expertise;
- Small firms often have different and less aggressive objectives than large businesses.

Considering that smaller firms are often founded on a particular product or technical skill of the owner, personalised as opposed to administrative approach to management is often adopted (Birley et al. 1999). Small firms also exhibit complex attitudes, behaviour and decision-making, depending on the personality of the owner-manager, where the responsibility for decision-making resides. Strategy formulation is essentially a top-down process, by which owners develop a strategic stance and ensure that their management and employees understand the strategy and behave in a manner commensurate with that strategy (Carson et al. 1995). As small business managers tend to be 'generalists' rather than 'specialists' in their business operations, decisions tend not to be made in isolation but in close connection with other aspects of the business (Carson and Gilmore 2000).

Large organisations, on the other hand, are inherently more complex in their organisation and structure; divided into more specialised departments with many layers of management (McAuley 2001).

While advantageous facets typically include close proximity to the market, differentiation and innovation (Nooteboom 1993; O'Gorman 2001), small firms encounter specific challenges defined as "resource constraint, and resource commitment, under conditions of uncertainty" (Erramilli and D'Souza 1993: 29). In terms of employment relationship, on one hand, the close proximity of owner-managers to employees generates informal and harmonious relations, characterised by good communication and greater flexibility (Bolton Report 1971; Ram and Edwards 2003). However, conversely there can be a greater propensity for problematic interpersonal relations in small firms, as sometimes owner managers are dictatorial and exploitative, and conflict is expressed through high levels of absenteeism and labour turnover (Sisson 1993; Barrett and Rainne 2002).

2.3.3 Variety

In general, the plant species host a range of familiar but varied organisms including trees, forbs, shrubs, grasses, vines, ferns, and mosses that live collectively within a designated community. In many ways small businesses, while more heterogeneous than homogenous (Bridge and O'Neill 2013), display distinct characteristics according to a specific 'variety' with common ancestry. For example, take the predominance of sole trader or self-employed business organisations in the UK of which there are 4.2 million (according to FSB 2016). This category of small business is less comparable to the initiators of new entrepreneurial ventures and closer to the status of employee. Often sole traders who run part time business are also full time employee of another firm (Bridge and O'Neill 2013).

Another distinct small firm is the family owned business, which make a major contribution to economics throughout the world (Hayworth 1992). Not restricted to the small business sector, family firms can be large as well as small. But, the ownership of family is not always translated into positive results. In fact, family feelings, values, and dynamics have been found to be a detrimental influence on business (Birley et al. 1999). The characteristic of ethnic ownership of small firms is another category as worthy of attention in the literature. According to Bridge and O'Neill (2013), this type of small firm is distinct due to nature of support structure (usually from a group socially distinguished by cultural or national origin), entrepreneurial activity (owners often engage in similar type of business activities), and employee recruitment (most often hire employees from the same ethnic group as well as source their customers).

As distinct as family and ethnicity, women ownership also exemplifies a specific variance of organisation within the small business sector. While there are a number of socio-economic issues that influence the prospects of small businesses founded by women, despite lacking initial resources (in comparison to male owners), it does not always mean these small businesses perform less well.

Acknowledging further variety within the small business sector e.g. academic spin out businesses (as a result of University knowledge transfer activity), high tech businesses (with significant economic contribution due to high growth potential), urban/rural businesses (issues of geographical accessibility), and third age businesses (started by people in middle age or retirement), this chapter cannot provide an exhaustive list of all firms. For a full discussion of the characteristics of these firms please read Chap. 5 of Bridge and O'Neill (2013).

2.4 Development and Growth

2.4.1 Life Cycle

The plant as a living organism starts life as a seed, germinates and grows into a plant, which corresponds largely to that of the business life cycle from conception to cessation. The business life cycle is often referred to in terms of stages such as sowing seeds, growing, pruning leaves, flowering as well as dying. Nevertheless, this linear stage of growth fails

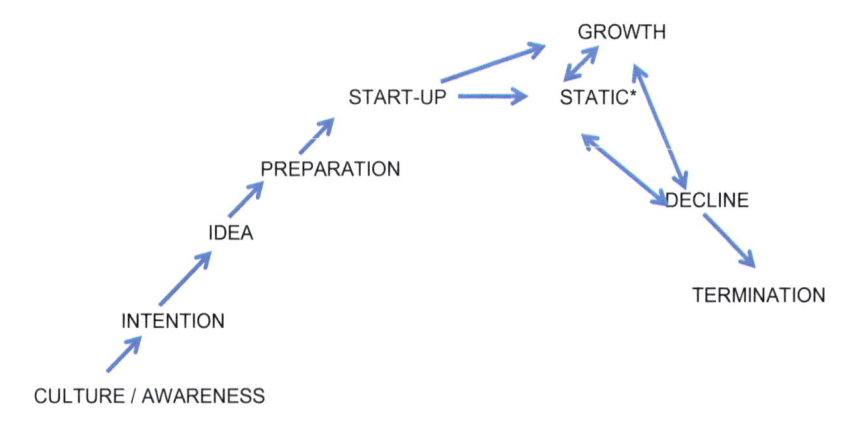

Fig. 2.1 Small business life cycle path. *Source* Adapted from Bridge and O'Neill (2013, p. 126). *Survival, consolidation, comfort and maturity

to fully capture the more ad hoc and less linear process of development for small businesses that do not necessarily progress through every stage. Some business can become static in growth and decline, progressing and reversing through stages in any order, as presented in Fig. 2.1.

Figure X is only one of many business life cycle models, but regardless it is important to note these models serve to present symptoms not causes of growth or decline at any given time, thereby failing to capture the internal conditions and reasons within the business (Bridge and O'Neill 2013).

It has been found that the entrepreneur or founder has an important influence upon the strategic and resource orientation, management structure, reward philosophy, growth orientation and entrepreneurial culture of a growing firm (Stevenson 1983). The Global Entrepreneurship Monitor specifically highlights the growing evidence of high impact entrepreneurs (Morris 2011) that lead businesses with above average impact in terms of growth evidenced by superior job creation, wealth creation and development of entrepreneurial role models. Ultimately, it is the ability and attitude of the owner to overcome barriers (whether internal and or external) that determines the actual growth potential of the business (O'Gorman 2001). These barriers change throughout the small business life cycle, requiring different type of support for the owner of the business (FSB 2016).

How owners organise the management of their small business has a significant impact on internal and external growth. At the early stage, start-ups tend to start off with a horizontal structure with an employee centred approach with few management layers, if any, and a wide span of authority. As the small business grows a traditional vertical structure consisting of strong management and subordinate employees may be adopted. On one hand, the shorter chain of command in horizontal organisations encourages transparency and enables faster decision-making faster as the business grows, facilitating employee engagement throughout the process of change. But, this type of flatter structure can also create frustration for employees, who may be less sure of their job role and have less room for upward career progression.

In the field of horticulture it was thought growth was a natural propensity for a plant, and if they didn't grow, it was due to external constraints such as lack of warmth and light, a drought or shortage of nutrients (Bridge and O'Neill 2013). But, recent research has revealed growth can also be constrained by internal inhibitors and therefore non-growth can also be normal (Bridge and O'Neill 2013). For instance, it has also been found that a lack of growth can be in the plant's longer-term interest preventing it from growing too fast for its conditions (Harberd 2007). For instance, one of the inhibitors internal to the business is located in the mind of the leader, the root that anchors the plant from storms. Lord Young (2013) refers to this influencing factor as a lack of confidence and strength of ambition in the business leader. Therefore, it doesn't matter what incentives exist in the external environment (or ecosystem as discussed in the next section) to help the business grow without the ambition and motivation from the leader, it will not happen (Bridge and O'Neill 2013).

2.4.2 Ecosystem

In order to fully understand the development and growth of plants, one must consider the whole ecosystem, that is the population of plant species plus its physical environment. In an ecosystem, species are on one hand interdependent on each other, yet, competitive enabling a healthy community of plant species. Equally, the relevance of the ecosystem is found in the field of business within the seminal works of Resource Based Theory and the work of Penrose (1959). One view refers to the ecosystem as the network of firms (Adner 2006), while others view it in a broader sense, to include education institutions, financial structures in the external environment (Sainsbury 2007), as well as the internal workings of the small business (Lubik and Garnsey 2014). As discussed in the previous section, the surrounding human society and culture is also critical for business growth, just as the condition and type of the soil are important for plants (Bridge and O'Neill 2013).

The characteristics of small firms relating to restricted finance, limited human resources, weak management and leadership skills, inability to influence the market, and inadequate planning procedures, can pose particular problems for growth. As such, the literature points to the resources and structures that generate a supportive ecosystem including government funding. For small firms, the rationale for policy intervention is to create a level playing field for small firms who encounter specific challenges compared to larger firms thereby circumventing market failure. In the case of academic spin-outs and new ventures, appropriate access to capital, realistic time horizons and diverse range of players has been found to help these firms realise their potential. Across the world, equity funding can be highly concentrated in specific geographical locations, such as the Silicon Valley in San Francisco, which are often cited as an exemplar of how to generate the ideal environment for high tech start-ups (Lubik and Garnsey 2014).

Financial investment is not the only type of critical intervention required for business life cycle; there is significant value in assisting owners with management and leadership skills development, strategic decision-making, as well as introductions and relationship building to facilitate and support growth ambition. It has been found that support for small businesses depends on the profile of the business and the stage of the business life cycle. According to the Federation of Small Business

(FSB 2016), the range of support schemes available to small firms can be categorised aligned to different stages of the life cycle.

For start-up businesses revenue is not always consistent therefore there is most often a short-term focus on survival. Access to finance is a particular challenge for small businesses and as Lubik and Garnsey (2014) explain there is a need for improvement in the flow of venture capital to small businesses in the early stage of growth. There is also a critical need for investment in addressing the mismatch between entrepreneurial activity and skills and capability required for growth (to be discussed in more detail in next chapter). The majority of firms in the small business sector are at the point of static growth, with potential to grow but lacking the drive or ambition to achieve it. For employing businesses, good human resource management skills are essential at this stage of growth, however, as is the case in most small businesses there is no dedicated HR function within the firm. Accounting for less than 1% of the total business population (NESTA 2009), high growth firms (believed to hold the key to job creation and wider prosperity) in specific priority sectors can avail of government support as well as investor funding such as equity finance that can also bring expertise and knowledge to improve performance.

But, ecosystems are constantly changing and the priority areas of government support at national and local levels can also vary. Companies fail for a variety of reasons including timing, lack of management skills, technological development, and cash flow (Lubik and Garnsey 2014). While challenges are most often sector specific, for small firms, building ecosystems with a sufficient variety of necessary players and resources to leverage is critical to survive and thrive (Lubik and Garnsey 2014). Chapter 3 will provide a more detailed discussion on the business support ecosystem specific to the development of leadership and management skills.

2.4.3 Market Exchange

Plants produce their own food by a chemical process called photosynthesis, using water, carbon dioxide and the energy of sunlight, which are essential to survive and thrive. In the same way all small firms regardless of industry sector need to provide a product/service offering for a market, with a suitable price and promotional message. This necessitates an essential and fundamental market exchange in order to survive and thrive. But, given the resource constraints inherent with small businesses, marketing planning, execution, and management as functions can be problematic for owner managers. The personal and individual style of management in small businesses means the owner both develops the marketing strategy and implements the marketing activities of the firm (Stokes and Nelson 2013). As a result, the personal experience, skills and attitudes of the owner manager are a major influencing factor in the way that marketing is perceived and carried out, which can be positive or negative influence on business performance.

Academic interest in the commonalities, differences and interface between small business marketing and entrepreneurship has evolved and developed over the past thirty years (Gilmore et al. 2013) resulting in the emerging area of entrepreneurial marketing thought. Research in this area contends that successful marketing is undertaken by firms who identify new opportunities, apply innovative techniques to successfully bring the product/service to meet the needs of their chosen target market and customers (Collinson and Shaw 2001). In this way, marketing communications tend to be more personalised and interactive relying on Word of Mouth recommendations and personal selling for positive and rewarding market exchange (Stokes 2000). Like the pollination of flowering plants, the effectiveness of marketing is most often highly dependent on networking (Gilmore and Carson 1999; Gilmore et al. 2001; Collinson and Shaw 2001; Miller et al. 2007) and the opportunities it provides for social capital (Shaw 2006). The networks of owner managers can facilitate the formation and generation of new and profitable customer exchange whereas Word of Mouth recommendations are facilitated through use of inter-organisational network relationships and personal contact networks (Gilmore et al. 2001; Hill and Wright 2001).

2.5 Chapter Summary

The focus of discussion in this chapter has been the small business organisation and why it is distinct from larger organisations. Notwithstanding full text books devoted to the small business organisation as an academic subject, the discussion herein provides an overview of the contribution, key defining characteristics, as well as the development and growth of these types of firms. Adopting the world of plants as a metaphor for the narrative, the discussion seeks to make the small business concept accessible to range of undergraduate, postgraduate students from a wide range of disciplines including those outside the business management domain. Defying the assumption that the only way to understand small business and their contribution to wealth creation is to focus on the organisation, the next chapter will place a microscope on the owner of the business and their leadership capacity as the X factor for survival and growth.

References

Adner, R. 2006. Match your innovation strategy to your innovation ecosystem. *Harvard Business Review* 84 (4) April: 98–107.

Aldrich, H.E. 1992. Incommensurable paradigms? Vital signs from three perspectives. In *Rethinking organisations: New directions in organisation theory and analysis,* ed. M. Reed and M. Hughes, 16–46. London: Sage.

Barnes, S., S. Kempster, and S. Smith. 2015. *LEADing small business: Business growth through leadership development.* London: Edward Elgar Publishing Ltd.

Barrett, R., and A. Rainnie. 2002. What's so special about small firms? Developing an integrated approach to analysing small firm industrial relations. *Work, Employment & Society* 16 (3): 415–432.

Birley, S., D. Ng, and A. Godfrey. 1999. The family and the business. *Long Range Planning* 32 (6): 598–608.

Bolton Report. 1971. *Small firms: Report of the committee of inquiry on small firms,* chaired by J.E. Bolton, CMND, 4811, HMSO, London.

Bridge, S., and K. O'Neill. 2013. *Understanding enterprise: Entrepreneurship and small business*, 4th ed. Basingstoke: Palgrave Macmillan.

Broadbridge, A., and E. Parsons. 2003. UK charity retailing: Managing in a newly professionalised sector. *Journal of Marketing Management* 19: 729–748.

Cardon, M.S., C. Zietsma, P. Saparito, P. Brett, P. Matherne, and C. Davis. 2005. "A tale of passion: New insights into entrepreneurship from a parenthood metaphor" original research article. *Journal of Business Venturing* 20 (1): 23–45.

Carson, D., S. Cromie, P. McGowan, and J. Hill. 1995. *Marketing and entrepreneurship in SMEs*. London: Prentice Hall.

Carson, D., and A. Gilmore. 2000. Marketing at the interface: Not 'what' but 'how'. *Journal of Marketing Theory and Practice* 8 (2): 1–8.

Collinson, E., and E. Shaw. 2001. Entrepreneurial marketing—A historical perspective on development and practice. *Management Decision* 39 (9): 761–766.

Cummins, S., and S. Macintyre. 2002. "Food deserts"—Evidence and assumption in health policy making. *British Medical Journal* 325: 436–438.

Davis, C.D., G.E. Hills, and R.W. LaForge. 1985. The marketing/small enterprise paradox: A research agenda. *International Small Business Journal* 3 (3): 31–42.

Erramilli, M.K., and D.E. D'Souza. 1993. Venturing into foreign markets: The case of the small service firm. *Entrepreneurship Theory and Practice* 17 (4): 29–41.

EU Commission. 2009. Online available at: http://ec.europa.eu/growth/smes/business-friendly-environment/sme-definition_en.

Federation of Small Business. 2016. Accessed https://www.fsb.org.uk/media-centre/small-business-statist.

Friedman, E. 2016. Why you need a small business metaphor. 3 July, Available: https://learn.infusionsoft.com/marketing/branding/why-you-need-a-small-business-metaphor.

Fuller, T. 2001. Small business futures in society. *Futures* 35: 297–304.

Gentner, D., and M. Jeziorski. 1993. The shift from metaphor to analogy in western science. In *Metaphor and thought,* 2nd ed., ed. A. Ortony, 447–480.

Gilmore, A., and D. Carson. 1999. Entrepreneurial marketing by networking. *New England Journal of Entrepreneurship* 12 (2): 31–38.

Gilmore, A., D. Carson, and K. Grant. 2001. SME marketing in practice. *Marketing Intelligence and Planning* 19 (1): 6–11.

Gilmore, A., McAuley, A., Gallagher, D., Massiera, P., Gamble, J. 2013. Researching SME/entrepreneurial research: A study of Journal of Research in Marketing and Entrepreneurship(JRME) 2000-2011. *Journal of Research in Marketing and Entrepreneurship* 15 (2): 87–100.

Harberd, N. 2007. *Seed to seed*, 302. London: Bloomsbury.

Hayworth, S. 1992. *The Stoy Hayward/BBC family business index*. London: Stoy Hayward.

Hill, J., and L.T. Wright. 2001. A qualitative research agenda for small to medium sized enterprises. *Marketing Intelligence and Planning* 19 (6): 432–443.

Krogue, K. 2012. 5 things business can learn from a tree. 11 December. Available at: https://www.forbes.com/sites/kenkrogue/2012/12/11/5-things-business-can-learn-from-a-tree/#3cd8d7c42265.

Lakoff, G., and M. Johnson. 1980. *Metaphors we live by*. Chicago: The University of Chicago Press.

Longworth, J. 2014. Small businesses are the backbone of our communities. *The Guardian*, Saturday 6 December.

Lubik, S., and E. Garnsey. 2014. Chapter 17: Entrepreneurial innovation in science-based firms: The need for an ecosystem perspective Sarah Lubik and Elizabeth Garnsey, 599–633.

Marshall, A. 1925. *Principles of economics*, 8th ed. London: Macmillan.

McAuley, A. 2001. *International marketing*. Chichester, United Kingdom: Wiley.

Miller, N.J., T. Besser, and A. Malshe. 2007. Strategic networking among small businesses in small US communities. *International Small Business Journal* 25 (6): 631–665.

Morris, R. 2011. *2011 High impact entrepreneurship global report*. Center for High-Impact Entrepreneurship at Endeavour and Global Entrepreneurship Monitor.

NESTA. 2009. The Vital 6 per cent, How high-growth innovative business generate prosperity and jobs. Available at http://www.nesta.org.uk/library/documents/Vitalsix-per-cent-Nov2010-v3.pdf.

Nooteboom, B. 1993. Firm size effects on transaction costs. *Small Business Economics* 5: 283–295.

O'Gorman, C. 2001. The sustainability of growth in small and medium-sized enterprises. *International Journal of Entrepreneurial Behaviour and Research* 7 (2): 60–75.

Paliwoda, S.J., and M.J. Thomas. 1998. *International marketing*. Oxford: Butterworth-Heinemann.

Penrose, E. 1959. *The theory of the growth of the firm*. Oxford: Oxford University Press.

Ram, M., and P. Edwards. 2003. Praising Caesar not burying him. *Work, Employment & Society* 17: 719–730.

Sainsbury, L. 2007. *The race to the top: A review of government's science and innovation policies*. Norwich: HM Treasury.

Shaw, E. 2006. Small firm networking: An insight into contents and motivating factors. *International Small Business Journal* 24 (1): 5–29.

Sisson, K. 1993. In search of HRM. *British Journal of Industrial Relations* 31 (2): 201–210.

Skorczynska, H. 2014. Metaphor and education: Reaching business training goals through multimodal metaphor. *Procedia—Social and Behavioral Sciences* 116: 2344–2351.

Stevenson, H.H. 1983. A perspective on entrepreneurship. *Harvard Business School Working Paper* 9: 384–131.

Stokes, D., and C.H. Nelson. 2013. Word of mouth to word of mouse: Social media and the entrepreneur. In *Entrepreneurial marketing, global perspectives*, ed. Z. Sethna, R. Jones, and P. Harrigan, 243–258. Emerald: Bingley.

Storey, D.J. 1994. *Understanding the small business sector*. New York: Routledge.

Valdiserri, G.A., and J. Wilson. 2010. The study of leadership in small business organisations: Impact on profitability and organisational success. *Entrepreneurial Executive* 15: 1087–8955.

White, M. 2003. *Metaphor and economics: The case of growth*. English for Specific Purposes 22: 131–151.

Wrigley, N., Warm, D., Margetts, B., Whelan, A. 2002. Assessing the Impact of Improved Retail Access on Diet in a 'Food Desert': A Preliminary Report. *Urban Studies* 39 (11): 2061–2082.

Young, Lord. 2013. *Growing your business: A report on micro firms*, May 2013. BIS/13/729, Crown copyright.

3
Leadership in Small Firms—The X Factor

Abstract The purpose of this chapter is to explore the importance of leadership in small business, which has been identified as the X factor for survival and growth (Barnes et al. 2015). While there is merit in understanding the distinctiveness of the small business organisation (Chap. 2), there is a greater need to understand the pivotal role of the owner in order to make sense of the whole story. Taking into account the different aspirations of business owners, Hutchinson provides a much needed and detailed discussion of the leadership capability of small firm leaders encompassing entrepreneurial leadership theory, alongside the rationale for intervention measures that improves organisational and economic impact.

Keywords Small business · Leadership theory · Entrepreneurial leadership · Small business owner · Leader · Motivations · X factor Business impact · Interventions · Economic productivity · Leadership training and development · Barriers · FSB · UKCES

3.1 Introduction

Until the 1990s, the primary focus of analysis in the small business literature was the firm, not the entrepreneur (Bridge and O'Neill 2013). While indicative of prolific reports commissioned by the government in the 1970s (e.g. The Bolton Report), various authors have since challenged the focus on the organisation. Most notably Gibb (1988), Scott and Rosa (1996), and Bridge and O'Neill (2013) argue since the business personifies the value system of owner, the process of wealth creation for the small firm is in fact owner/entrepreneur led. Since the 1990s, it became clear that leadership in larger and more established organisations couldn't be transposed into the small business context. Yet, research focused on leadership as a concept and endeavour in the general field of small business management has been limited. Research in the new and emerging area of 'Entrepreneurial Leadership' on the other hand has extended this debate by focusing on the specifics of leadership in new and existing small organisations, which offers a valuable source of insight for the purpose of this book.

Leadership has been a major topic of research in psychology and management for almost a century involving thousands of empirical and conceptual studies (Leitch and Volery 2017). But, to better understand the concept of small business leadership, the next section will present current debate within the domain of small business management, albeit limited in scope and depth of study. A more detailed discussion of the definition and characteristics of entrepreneurial leadership will be provided in the subsequent section, which will review emerging academic thinking relevant to wide range of small businesses. Thereafter, the chapter will progress the discussion to take account of the correlation between leadership and business as well as economic impact. It is this connection that underpins the rationale for intervention measures in the form of leadership development programmes and support, to be fully explained in the latter sections of this chapter.

3.2 Study of Leadership in Small Business Management

Notwithstanding the plethora of leadership definitions and theoretical models in wider management literature, there is a lack of academic understanding of what constitutes leadership in the context of the small business organisation. Characterised by one-person centred organisational structure and highly personal approach to management (reflecting not only personal goals but those of the family), the owners of small business organisations are intrinsically different in their approach to leading, solving business problems, learning, and making decisions compared to larger businesses. Appreciating that in the literature small business failures are associated with poor leadership (Perry 2001; Beaver 2003), it has been found that effective leadership defined by transformational and transactional styles have a significant impact on organisational profitability and success (Valdiserri and Wilson 2010). Yet, in reality, leadership is often considered an irrelevant concept to the small business owner even though they are "doing" leadership everyday (Barnes et al. 2015).

Inside a small firm, the owner is most often all-powerful, but not always prone to make decisions based on sound business reasoning. Since "*the business is not only the creation of the person, but is also the expression of the person*" (Bridge and O'Neill 2013: 179), decisions are often made for personal, not commercial reasons. But, it would be incorrect to generalise the motivation for decision-making across the small business sector. The fact of the matter is not all small business owners are equally entrepreneurial or indeed entrepreneurial at all. Different type of owners will have different traits and behaviour, as well as distinct motivations for the business. In order to understand the different motivations of small business owners, three main categories are proposed by Hornaday (1990) including:

1. Craftsman: practices a trade, craft or occupation, with few if any employees.
2. Professional manager: builds an adaptive organisation over time.

3. Entrepreneur: creates and develops a firm as the pursuit of personal wealth and presentation of new products and invention.

While this categorisation of ownership was developed some years ago, it still provides a relevant basis for understanding leadership in a small business context. Building on this, Bridge and O'Neill (2013: 180) suggests three broad categories of small business owners' motivation, which include:

1. Lifestyle: the owner seeks to run a business that not only facilitates, but is part of the lifestyle the owner wants to have, this could include for example a part-time business.
2. Comfort-zone: the owner seeks sufficient returns from a business for the level of comfort in life, where the basis of the business is less important than the level of benefit it can provide for a reasonable amount of effort.
3. Growth: the owner seeks to manage the business to increase its wealth generation either with a 'professional' motivation to build the organisation to maximise future earnings, or the 'entrepreneur' motivation to maximise personal wealth.

In reality, many owners of small business perceive success as reaching a level of comfort rather than achieving the full potential of the business, aligned to motivations within the lifestyle and comfort-zone categories. In other words, not all small business owners desire to grow their business, especially if it involves more effort or puts the comfort zone at risk. One of the underlying reasons is the integration of the business and non-business life of small firm owners whereby the business is viewed in terms of life as a whole including family and friends. Therefore, as Bridge and O'Neill (2013) rightly point out, the relatively low productivity in small business sector may not be the result of the failure of management, but due to a different vision and set of motivations by the owner. As Chaps. 4 and 5 will go on to explain, the leadership purpose of the small business is critical for the development of the firm, which is underpinned by Pink's (2010) argument that often business owners are purpose maximisers, not just profit maximers. So, as Bridge and O'Neill (2013) explain, in order to fully understand the intentions of small business owners, it is necessary to ascertain what their purposes are, and for many leaders in this sector, this can incorporate a sense of social purpose.

Entrepreneurial owners of small businesses are distinct in terms of their motivations and are likely to fall within the growth (or high growth) category previously discussed. Specific attention has been dedicated to entrepreneurial leadership as an emerging a field of study; therefore, the following section will examine existing knowledge on the subject in order to present additional discussion around defining leadership in a small business context.

3.3 Entrepreneurial Leadership

Given the increasingly turbulent and competitive environment, as well as the ineffectiveness of more traditional approaches to strategy, the 1990s gave way to a type of "entrepreneurial" leader distinct from other behavioural forms of leadership (Gupta et al. 2004). Since then, there has been a significant growth in this area, especially since it emerged that previous research in larger and more established organisations couldn't be transposed into the small business context (Leitch and Volery 2017). Entrepreneurial leadership as an area of academic enquiry takes into consideration the specifics of leadership in new and existing small organisations, not only those firms operating in highly competitive and dynamic environments. This category of leadership is not specific to any type of organisation, industry or culture, but rather can flourish in a wide range of enterprises (Renko et al. 2013). Indeed, the importance of incorporating an entrepreneurial mindset is now recognised as a core element of strategic management in organisations of any size and sector (McGrath and MacMillan 2000). Although entrepreneurial leadership is embraced in the popular press and in classrooms, academic knowledge remains somewhat underdeveloped (Renko et al. 2013).

3.3.1 Theoretical Intersection

The starting point of understanding entrepreneurial leadership can be found either in the field of leadership or entrepreneurship. There are various views on the positioning of theoretical understanding in this area. On one hand, behaviours traditionally associated with entrepreneurship have been integrated into mainstream leadership literature to the extent to which entrepreneurial behaviour has become the essence of leadership (Leitch and Volery 2017). In other words, the emphasis on a new generation of leadership known by their high risk-taking, opportunity seeking and advantage-seeking behaviour (Nicholson 1998; Ireland et al. 2003) is paramount for the navigating the turbulence of the present day economy. Therefore, for some authors, entrepreneurial leadership is not necessarily distinct (Vecchio 2003), but rather is a type of leadership that occurs in a specific setting such as in small fast growing businesses "capable of sustaining innovation and adaptation in high-velocity and uncertain environments" (Gupta et al. 2004: 245).

Leadership theory has been translated to the field of entrepreneurial leadership to assist the understanding of the ability of entrepreneurial leaders to influence a group of followers:

- Transformational leadership: the ability of entrepreneurial leader to evoke superordinate performance is founded in the context of the firm's need to adapt to emerging environmental contingencies.
- Team-orientated leadership: the ability of leaders to elicit heightened levels of group participation and involvement in the leader-team exchange in an uncertain organisational context.
- Value-based leadership: the entrepreneurial leader's capacity to build a high-expectation vision while relying on the commitment of followers to use their specialised skills to accomplish the vision (Gupta et al. 2004).

A different perspective considers entrepreneurial leadership as a new paradigm, which explores common themes and linkages between both fields of study mutually benefiting from the cross-fertilisation (Leitch and Volery 2017). A summary is presented in Table 3.1.

Table 3.1 Entrepreneurial leadership as a new paradigm

Perspective	Explanation	Author/s
Ontological	Entrepreneur is leader—leadership is a core component of the entrepreneurial process	Fernald et al. (2005), Kempster and Cope (2010)
Personal characteristics/traits	Effectiveness linked to persistence, creativity, enthusiasm, risk-taking, proactiveness and innovativeness	Chen (2007), Kempster and Cope (2010)
Style	Characterised by authentic, charismatic and transformational leadership able to inspire and energise followers	Jensen and Luthans (2006)

Source Adapted from Leitch and Volery (2017)

While there is sound rationale for justifying this as a new and distinct academic field, others raise the question whether entrepreneurial leadership is truly a new style of leadership, or an escape from management, or both (Fernald et al. 2005)? But, according to Leitch and Volery (2017) evolution continues in this area, marked by new shift from a focus on personal characteristics and traits to role and behaviour defined by interaction within specific contexts. This in turn has seen a second shift in emphasis from static, descriptive analyses to a more dynamic view of entrepreneurial leadership including leadership development (e.g. Leitch et al. 2009).

3.3.2 Characteristics of Entrepreneurial Leaders

Both leaders and entrepreneurs have been studied relative to their traits, skills, and behavioral characteristics in an attempt to define a successful leader or entrepreneur (Fernald et al. 2005). Entrepreneurial thinking is most often associated with the leaders of new ventures, defined by opportunity seeking, achievement striving, risk bearing, and proactive behaviour in complex and volatile environments (Nicholson 1998; Gupta et al. 2004). Many studies have shown that entrepreneurs have higher comfort with risk than conventional managers, in that they are better at living with it and managing the anxiety that might be disabling to others (Butler 2017). Often described as innovators, paradigm pioneers, and visionaries, entrepreneurs are confronted with the challenge of developing leadership qualities in order to grow their businesses and adopt greater professionalism in their approach to doing business. Nicholson (1998) in his study of small to medium-sized independent firms, defined entrepreneurial leaders as tough-minded people, indifferent to social distractions, not diverted by curiosity, and driven by a need for active dominance.

In reality, what sets entrepreneurial leaders apart from other small business leaders is the ability to thrive in uncertainty. This requires an openness to new experiences, which not only entails a willingness to proceed in unpredictable environments, but a heightened state of motivation at the edge of the unknown and the untried (Butler 2017). Indeed, it is argued that the organisational archetype of the future will be entrepreneurial. This reflects the definition provided by Leitch et al. (2013, 348), which contends it is *"leadership role performed in entrepreneurial ventures, rather than in the more general sense of an entrepreneurial style of leadership"*. The characteristics and behaviours that spell success in entrepreneurial firms and small businesses are now considered just as vital for large transnational corporations. Therefore, in progressing understanding of leadership in small firms, entrepreneurial leadership cannot be limited to new ventures or to firms operating in highly competitive and dynamic environments. No matter, it is certainly the necessary state for success and growth for small business organisations.

3.4 Leadership Impact and Intervention

In order to appreciate the X factor of growth and success for small firms, the following sections will focus on the impact of leadership at a wider economic level, as well as at a micro organisational level. In understanding the challenges to realising and mobilising leadership potential, this discussion will also provide some insight into the role of intervention by government and business support organisations.

3.4.1 Economic Productivity and Ambition Debate

It is widely accepted that the productivity of the economy is negatively affected by weaknesses in leadership and management capabilities and specifically in the small business sector (BIS 2012; CMI 2015; UKCES 2015b; FSB 2016). Not only are leadership and management skills relatively underdeveloped in many small firms (BIS 2015), but combined with a widespread failure to adopt management practices, the performance of a large number of small firms in the UK is no doubt inhibited (UKCES 2015a). This is likewise the case in economic terms for the US, where it has also been found that the primary cause of small business failures was management incompetence (Beaver 2003). The skills most strongly associated with high quality management practice and small firm performance and growth, are entrepreneurship skills (identifying customer needs, technical or market opportunities, and pursuing opportunities), and leadership skills (motivating and influencing others and delegating work) (UKCES 2015a). According to Barnes et al. (2015), if these practices were fully implemented by small firms then the growth and impact in the economy would be considerable.

In order for small businesses to affect the change required for economic impact, the owner must first want to grow (i.e. have a strength of ambition), and then be able to plan and resource that growth (i.e. acquire the necessary leadership and management skills). There is a very small percentage (less than 1% of established businesses) of high growth SMEs that generate 20% of all UK job growth (Goldman Sachs 2015). Indeed, there is evidence of a clear 'growth ambition gap' by leaders across the small business sector in the UK compared to other G8 economies. This point was also made by Lord Young (2013), which argued that ambitious small businesses were the most likely to grow in terms of turnover and employment. While the majority of small business owners assert they want to grow, relatively few achieve this in practice. In reality, fewer small business owners have a substantive ambition to grow, that is a desire to grow met with determination, opportunity and a strong level of leadership and management to make it happen (Lord Young 2013). In order to close the gap, the Goldman Sachs Report (2015) recommends improvements in the entrepreneurial ecosystem to help build this growth ambition with improved access to capital and expanded business education identified as critical enablers.

As previously explained, there will always be "lifestyle" firms with little or no growth ambition, but there are other small firms that do not grow but are well placed to do so. According to Goldman Sachs (2015), there are more than 110,000 UK small firms with the potential either to start exporting or expand their existing exports, yet do not. These small businesses experiencing static growth could include firms that have downsized due to the recession with a strong desire to grow back to previous levels, or the owners of small firms who are have strong growth aspirations but little awareness of the opportunity and help available to make it happen. Indeed, small business owners must be prepared to overcome the leadership and management challenges that come with growing a business, whether practical or psychological and be able to navigate the dense waters of business support to find the right intervention. These factors will be discussed later.

3.4.2 Business Impact

Large businesses may be able to survive for short periods without great leadership in place, but the opposite is true for small businesses. Comprised of few employees and some without any, the small business quickly falls apart without strong leadership purpose and capability. Take for instance, the high failure of small businesses. According to research by the CMI (2015) the survival rate of UK businesses in the first 5 years is only 56%, which is the majority of new firms. Moreover, significant regional variations such as in Northern Ireland, there are the lower than average rates of both creation and survival of start-ups at 49%. The most cited reason for failure is the lack of management and leadership competence. Why? Leadership and management skills are required to organise the resources that operate the business, therefore non-performance of leadership responsibilities demonstrates the leader's inability to achieve profitability and success, which ultimately leads to failure.

The business benefits of high quality leadership and management are many. Since, the small business leader lays the foundation of the firm's culture, he or she is responsible for creating and communicating the purpose of the business and ensuring the team understands the difficulties and challenges. But, the leader must also ensure employees have the desire and capability to manage problems and challenges that are encountered by the firm, which depends on the recruiting and managing the right team of staff. These type of strong and effective management practices do not just result in higher productivity, but yield better returns on capital and more robust growth for the small business (FSB 2016). The question of how small business owners can create the right conditions for realising growth potential was the focus of Lord Young's Report (2013). This report pointed to the influence of leadership ability, as well as the importance of relevant and accessible business support relating to confidence, capability, and coherence of support.

Small business leaders establish the working atmosphere of their business through their leadership style, which permeates the functionality and performance of all operations (Valdiserri and Wilson 2010). Indeed, the centrality of the owner to the business means small firms are dependent on the owner's insight, skills, training, education and characteristics. The characteristics of the owner and business influence the required mix of knowledge and skills for effective management and leadership, as well as how management and leadership capacity for learning might best be developed (UKCES 2015b). A combination of leadership and entrepreneurship skills are positively related to strategy formulation and responsiveness, and fundamental drivers of performance and growth (BIS 2015). Yet, despite the direct correlation between the owner manager's skills and the ability of small firms to survive and thrive, the leaders of these organisations undertake less training and development than bigger firms (FSB 2016).

The acquisition and embedding of new knowledge by the small business owner for wider impact is considered critical for enhancing performance (Jones et al. 2010). This 'how' of small business leadership learning and development has attracted attention in the literature and will be addressed in greater detail in Chap. 6, where the author's Lead2Grow model for small business is presented and explained.

3.4.3 Barriers to Leadership Training and Development

Notwithstanding the positive impact of effective leadership at economic and business levels, there are barriers that often prevent the realisation of these benefits for the small business. It is recognised that small firms encounter unique challenges in leading, distinct from larger business organisations with functional divisions of labour (as discussed in Chap. 2). The first relates to the perception of the term leadership. In many cases the owners of small businesses don't view themselves as leaders (CMI 2015). According to Kempster (2009) there is a low recognition of the leadership phenomenon and weak desire to study it, despite evidence of strong forms of leadership by successful small firms. Moreover, in micro firms, the task of management is often embodied within a single individual responsible for all major functions. These individuals are perhaps more likely to self-identify as 'business people' rather than as professional managers (Devins et al. 2005). Secondly, many small firm owners are too busy working in the business to take time to work on the business. Indeed, most small business owners find it difficult to remove themselves from the operational concerns of the business to focus on strategy, therefore the key challenge for small business leader is to either work "in" or "on" the business (Barnes et al. 2015).

Thirdly, owners are most often competent and knowledgeable with regards to their specific business activities and their pursuit of value-generating opportunities (e.g. Rae and Carswell 2000), but often lack more generic leadership, managerial and administrative capabilities such as those related to finance, staff, sales and marketing, legal or other functions (Goffee and Scase 1995). Particularly at micro-levels of scale, business owners can possess limited managerial skills and fail to operate a sophisticated management structure. As a result, owner manager's management and administrative capabilities are often hindered by their reluctance to delegate decision-making authority, recruit managers with dedicated responsibilities (Rae and Carswell 2001), or train existing staff.

Fourthly, many owner-managers do not possess formal educational qualifications and lack any specific formal training, relying largely on prior employment and managerial experience, and their own experiential learning on-the-job to provide them with the managerial knowledge and skills they use to operate their businesses (UKCES 2015a). These leaders often draw on early formative experiences such as family, education and first jobs, as opposed to taking part in leadership development programmes, therefore the small business is often the crucible where owners learn to lead (Bennis and Thomas 2002). But, external knowledge is a significant source of learning for the small firm, with profound impact if incorporated with the existing knowledge of the owner manager (Jones et al. 2010). The question of how this leadership learning can translate into real business impact will be discussed in Chap. 6.

The final barrier to engaging in leadership development training programmes is the growth challenge. The FSB (2016) explores the prioritisation of leadership and management skills at three key stages of the business life cycle- starting up, growing moderately, and high growth. Each phase of growth presents new and different management and leadership challenges to a small business:

- Start-up: the survival rates of UK businesses in the first 5 years are lower than France and Germany (Eurostat 2012). Not just about financing, but access to a broader business support in order to address the mismatch between entrepreneurial activity and skills and capabilities required for growth. While there is a vast number of programmes available, it is found that more often informal support such as peer networks and mentoring contributes to firm growth.
- Moderate growers: largest proportion of businesses who have been established for more than 5 years and experience consistent trading or 'static growth'. Some may be operating in markets that lack competitive pressure, so the focus of additional support must be firm with the potential to grow but lack knowledge and skills to make it happen. For small firms with employees, good human resource management skills are also critical to bring in new staff and boost workforce productivity (BIS 2015), yet many small and micro businesses do not have a dedicated HR function within the firm.
- High growth firms: those who want to grow in terms of product/service and people. But these businesses account for less than 1% of business population. For these high growth firms, require support in the form of equity finance bringing people/expertise and funding.

Crossing the gap from the 'one-man-band' entrepreneurial business to an organised, well-managed enterprise with employees is the biggest single challenge for many owners. In a growing business where the owner experiences pressures to delegate authority, there might be a lack of willingness to distribute leadership functions to others because it undermines their sense of 'being entrepreneurial' (Cope et al. 2011). For growth-ambivalent business owners the Goldman Sachs Report (2015) defines a more 'opportunistic' or 'ad hoc' in their approach to growth, lacking the leadership ability to explore or exploit the full range of possibilities open to the business at a strategic level. There are also psychological barriers associated with navigating regulations, hiring staff or exporting (Lord Young 2013), which discourage small business leaders from taking growth plans forward. Some owners may feel isolated in dealing with the challenges of growth into unknown and unchartered territories, which can be extremely daunting. Therefore, these leaders instead remain too focused on short-term concerns such as cash flow, clients, suppliers and recruitment, distracted from long-term goals (CMI 2015).

3.4.4 Interventions in the Ecosystem

The benefits are obvious, the wider economic impact convincing, and the challenges formidable. In the business support ecosystem, there is a plethora of intervention measures designed to help overcome the challenges to improve the leadership and management skills of small businesses. In fact, there are over 600 different business growth support programmes available to small firms in the UK (Goldman Sachs 2015). Despite the significant supply of leadership and entrepreneurship support available in the market for small firms to access, the UK still has a long tail of small firms who do not engage. According to UKCES (2015a), only 33% of small firms access any management training, so for whatever reason the market is not providing what small firms require. Some note small business managers find the landscape complex, confusing and time-consuming to navigate (Barnes et al. 2015). According to Rae et al. (2012) the public provision has overall failed to provide either a sustained foundation for skills development in small firms or coherent evidence of impact. Thereby validating the critique offered a decade before by Storey (2004). So, while there have been a number of government schemes designed to improve SME growth through leadership development, there is still much to do in this arena (Smallbone et al. 2015).

The problems with existing support measures are well debated. Take for instance firm characteristics discussed in Chap. 2. The small firm population is highly diverse in terms of size, ownership, business activities and sector, nature and shape of markets, the relevance of product and process innovation, and growth intentions. Moreover, small firms in different sectors encounter different resource demands, minimum efficient scale requirements, market pressures to innovate, and workforce skill requirements, which all have significant implications for the leadership and managerial capabilities required to succeed (UKCES 2015b). Think about the range of sizes in the small business sector from the predominance of sole traders with no employees, to micro, small and medium sized firms with 250 employees. There is no doubt that size matters when it comes to leadership development programme design and delivery. Micro firms employing fewer than 10 staff, are less likely to manage functional divisions of labour and approach leadership in a more informal way, whereas medium sized firms are more likely to employ managers with dedicated responsibility for finance, employment, technical/operations, and sales and marketing (UKCES 2015a).

There is more recent research on the type of learning activities in training programmes, which point to management and leadership development as a situated and context-dependent activity arising from participation in planned and unplanned activities in the workplace and elsewhere. Traditional training programmes are often too broad or vague to be usefully applied in the real business world. Therefore, there is substantial evidence underlining the importance of on-the-job, experiential learning for owner-managers and employed managers arising from participation in working activities and from interaction with suppliers, customers, employees and others (UKCES 2015b). It is less about highly polished delivery and more about co-constructing leadership practice with business owners, placing emphasis on the connection between learning and personal/business context (Barnes et al. 2015). Chap. 6 will discuss the nature of leadership development and learning in more detail.

Notwithstanding the debates around leadership training and the return on investment for the business and funders (Bolden 2001), there has been sustained investment and commitment by various agencies as well as University Business Schools to see change and improvement. Examples include the LEAD programme based at Lancaster (Smith and Robinson 2007) as well as the launch of the Small Business Charter by Lord Young and the Department for Business, Innovation and Skills, with the Chartered Association of Business Schools. The Small Business Charter award gives business schools recognition for the far-reaching and innovative support they provide to SMEs, and for the impact they have on their local economies (Lord Young 2013). The CMI Report (2015) verifies improvement in small business productivity and survival through the application of business and management education. It also details how Business schools will also become a key part of the referral process and provision of Start-Up Loans and Growth Vouchers. According to FSB (2016), Growth Hubs, LEPs, provide environments, resources and facilities, which will help facilitate peer networks creating valuable channels for informing, raising awareness and encouraging best practice.

A public sector scheme by the UK Commission for Employment and Skills (UKCES) is noteworthy also as an exemplar of innovation in the ecosystem. The competitive call for research projects by the UKCES in 2105 to test out new ways of engaging with small firms, explored the extent to which anchor organisations, who currently play no major role in skills development, can use their influence to support small firms develop improved leadership and entrepreneurship skills. The author in working with a local agency was successful in securing funding for the design and delivery of the bespoke Lead2Grow programme for micro business leaders discussed later in this book.

A relatively new private-sector initiative is the Goldman Sachs '10,000 Small Businesses' programme. Hosted by four English universities, this scheme provides high-quality, practical support to the owners and leaders of established small businesses and social enterprises as they seek to grow. For the participants, the core of the program is a practically-focused business and management education, delivered over 12 sessions lasting a total of approximately 100 hours. During the course of the programme every small business owner develops a customised growth plan to direct their organisation's business strategy and expansion. The report published by Goldman Sachs (2015) echoes Lord Young's Report (2013) published 2 years prior in making the case for changes in the business ecosystem based on three key recommendations for future development:

1. Overall entrepreneurial ecosystem needs to be nurtured to encourage greater growth ambition among SMEs.
2. Need to expand and increase appropriate forms of education to help build the UK's entrepreneurial ecosystem: Practical and impactful business education for SMEs is fundamental in providing SMEs with the appetite to internationalise and innovate.
3. Capital is a critical enabler for SMEs to internationalise and innovate: Solutions focus on initiatives that stimulate demand and support supply through debt and equity financing.

These suggestions underpin the need for support that sees a cultural shift in the mindset of small business leaders, as well novel and collaborate learning interventions, with practical financial support, in order to see the benefits of leadership development in small firms mobilised in a sustainable way for real economic impact.

3.5 Chapter Summary

This chapter focused discussion on the small business leader who plays centre stage in the story set out in Chap. 2. There may be limited attention given to leadership and leadership development in the small business management literature, but the emerging domain of entrepreneurial leadership serves to provide insight into the distinct leadership characteristics and approach necessary for survival and growth given the turbulence and pace of change in global markets. While there is no doubt of the leadership X factor for small business, there are significant challenges to be overcome if the benefits and impact are to be achieved at a firm and economic level. Understanding that poor management is holding back growth and indeed is the leading cause of small business failure, there is a real imperative for improving management and leadership skills in small firms (CMI 2015). But, despite the sizeable ecosystem of business support in this area, and the fact "to lead is to learn", more must be done to encourage these leaders to invest in their own capability and skills to improve performance.

References

Barnes, S., S. Kempster, and S. Smith. 2015. *LEADing small business: Business growth through leadership development*. Cheltenham: Edward Elgar.

Beaver, G. 2003. Small business: Success and failure. *Strategic Change* 12 (3): 115–122.

Bennis, W. and Thomas, R. J. 2002. Crucibles of Leadership. *Harvard Business Review* 80 (9): 39–45.

Bolden, R. 2001. *Leadership development in small and medium sized enterprises: Final report*. Centre for Leadership Studies, University of Exeter, July 2001.

Bridge, S., and K. O'Neill. 2013. *Understanding enterprise: Entrepreneurship and small business*, 4th ed. New York: Palgrave Macmillan.

Butler, T. 2017. Hiring an entrepreneurial leader. *Harvard Business Review* 95 (2) March–April: 85–93.

Chen, M-H. 2007. Entrepreneurial Leadership and New Ventures: Creativity in Entrepreneurial Teams. *Creativity and Innovation Management* 16: 239–249.

CMI. 2015. *Growing your small business: The role of business schools and professional bodies*. London: Chartered Management Institute Publication, September.

Cope, J., S. Kempster, and K. Parry. 2011. Exploring distributed leadership in the small business context. *International Journal of Management Reviews* 13 (3): 270–285.

Department of Business Innovation and Skills (BIS). 2012. Fixing the foundations: Creating a more prosperous nation. Policy paper, 10 July.

Department of Business Innovation and Skills (BIS). 2015. Leadership and management skills in small and medium-sized businesses. Research paper, 3 March 2015, Ref: BIS/15/95.

Devins, D., J. Gold, S. Johnson, and R. Holden. 2005. A conceptual model of management learning in micro businesses: Implications for research and policy. *Education and Training* 47 (8/9): 540–551.

Eurostat, 2012. One, three and five year survival rates of enterprise.

Federation of Small Business. 2016. Leading the way: Boosting leadership and management in small firms. Discussion paper, March 2016.

Fernald, L.W., G.T. Solomon, and A. Tarabishy. 2005. A new paradigm: Entrepreneurial leadership. *Southern Business Review* 30 (2) Spring: 1–10.

Gibb, A.A. 1988. Towards the building of entrepreneurial models of support for small business. Paper presented at the 11th national small firm's policy and research conference, Cardiff.

Goffee, R., and R. Scase. 1995. *Corporate realities: The dynamics of large and small firms*. London: International Thompson Business Press.

Goldman Sachs. 2015. Unlocking UK productivity—Internationalisation and innovation in SMEs. *Goldman Sachs 10,000 Businesses*. Online available at: http://www.goldmansachs.com/citizenship/10000-small-businesses/UK/news-and-events/gew-2015-f/unlocking-uk-productivity.pdf.

Gupta, V., I. MacMillan, and G. Surie. 2004. Entrepreneurial leadership: Developing and measuring a cross-cultural construct. *Journal of Business Venturing* 19: 241–260.

Hornaday, R.W. 1990. Dropping the E-word from small business research. *Journal of Small Business Management* 28 (4): 22–33.

Ireland, R.D., M.A. Hitt, D.G. Sirmon. 2003. A model of strategic entrepreneurship: The construct and its dimensions. *Journal of Management* 29 (6): 963–989.

Jensen, S. M., and Luthans, F. 2006. Entrepreneurs as authentic leaders: Impact on employees' attitudes. *Leadership and Organizational Development Journal* 27(8): 646.

Jones, O., A. Macpherson, and R. Thorpe. 2010. Learning in owner-managed small firms: Mediating artefacts and strategic space. *Entrepreneurship and Regional Development* 22 (7): 649–673.

Kempster 2009. "Observing the Invisible: Examining the Role of Observational Learning in the Development of Leadership Practice." *Journal of Management Development* 28, 5: 439–456.

Kempster, S., and J. Cope. 2010. Learning to lead in the entrepreneurial context. *International Journal of Entrepreneurial Behaviour and Research* 16 (1): 5–34.

Leitch, C., and T. Volery. 2017. Entrepreneurial leadership: Insights and directions. *International Small Business Journal* 35 (2): 147–156.

Leitch, C., C. McMullan, and R.T. Harrison. 2009. Leadership development in SMES: An action learning approach. *Action Learning: Research and Practice* 6 (3): 243–263.

Leitch, Claire M., Christel McMullan, and Richard T. Harrison. 2013. The development of entrepreneurial leadership: The role of human, social and institutional capital. *British Journal of Management* 24 (3): 347–366.

McGrath, R.G., and I.C. MacMillan. 2000. *The entrepreneurial mindset*. Boston, MA: Harvard Business School Press.

Nicholson, N. 1998. Personality and entrepreneurial leadership: A study of the heads of the UK's most successful independent companies. *European Management Journal* 16 (5): 529–539.

Perry, C.S. 2001. The relationship between written business plans and the failure of small businesses in the US. *Journal of Small Business Management* 39: 201–209.

Pink, D. 2010. Gainful employment. *RSA Journal* 156 (Spring): 26–29.

Rae, D. and Carswell, M. 2000. Using a life-story approach in entrepreneurial learning: The development of a conceptual model and its implications in the design of learning experiences. *Education and Training* 42, 220–227.

Rae, D., and M. Carswell. 2001. Towards a conceptual understanding of entrepreneurial learning. *Journal of Small Business and Enterprise Development* 8 (2): 150–158.

Rae, D., L. Price, G. Bosworth, and P. Parkinson. 2012. Business inspiration: Small business leadership in recovery? *Industry & Higher Education* 26 (6): 473–489.

Renko, M., A.E. Tarabishy, A.L. Carsud, and M. Brannback. 2013. Understanding and measuring entrepreneurial leadership style. *Journal of Small Business Management* 53 (1): 54–74.

Scott, M., and P. Rosa. 1996. Has firm level analysis reached its limits? Time for a rethink. *International Small Business Journal* 14 (4): 81–99.

Smallbone, D., J. Kitching, R. Blackburn, and S. Mosavi. 2015. *Anchor institutions and small firms in the UK*. Rotherham: UK Commission for Employment and Skills.

Smith, L., and S. Robinson. 2007. *Leading enterprise and development: Report on the design and delivery of a programme to engage and motivate small businesses in leadership and management development.* Lancaster: IEED, Lancaster University Management School.

Storey, D. 2004. Exploring the link among small firms, between training and firm performance: A comparison between UK and other OECD countries. *International Journal of Human Resource Management* 15 (1): 112–130.

UKCES. 2015a. *Developing leadership and entrepreneurship skills in small firms: How can anchor institutions support the development of small firms in their local economy?* Rotherham: UK Commission for Employment and Skills, March 2015.

UKCES. 2015b. *Anchor institutions and small firms in the UK: A review of the literature on anchor institutions and their role in developing management and leadership skills in small firms.* Rotherham: UK Commission for Employment and Skills, March.

Valdiserri, G.A., and J. Wilson. 2010. The study of leadership in small business organisations: Impact on profitability and organisational success. *Entrepreneurial Executive* 15, ISSN:1087-8955.

Vecchio, R.P. 2003. Entrepreneurship and leadership: Common trends and common threads. *Human Resource Management Review* 13: 303–327.

Young, Lord. 2013. *Growing your business: A report on micro firms*, May 2013. BIS/13/729, Crown copyright.

4

Leadership Purpose

Abstract In the saturated marketplace of leadership theories, Hutchinson explores the growing interest and relevance of the leadership purpose ethos for small business owners. Although the notion of 'purpose' is not a new one, academic research into leadership purpose for business is scarce and almost always told from the perspective of large multinational corporations. This chapter will discuss the roots of leadership purpose in authentic leadership theory as well as presenting the framework of leadership purpose. The latter sections will explore the practical relevance and benefits for the leaders of small business organisations.

Keywords Small business · Small business owner · Leader · Purpose driven leadership · Authentic leadership · Integration of purpose · Business impact

4.1 Introduction

For more than 80 years researchers and practitioners have recognised a vast array of leadership theories to help organisations identify, select and train leaders (Russell and Underwood 2016). A plethora of leadership books, thought leaders, leadership research articles, leadership theories, leadership seminars, and leadership development programmes are widely available. By illustration, type 'leadership books' into the Amazon.com search engine and over 200,000 titles are listed! It is a hot topic because it's important and because traditional leadership qualities and strategies are being challenged by new research telling us people respond to leadership differently than they used to. The expectations and thinking around what makes a good leader has changed on account of profound political and societal changes. Also significant, is the fact half of the millennial generation (people born in the 1980s to early 2000s) are already in leadership positions, exhibiting a distinct set of preferences and attitudes to leading and doing business (Bersin 2013).

The current chapter seeks to explore one of the newest areas of leadership research, purpose driven leadership (Craig and Snooks 2014), rooted in the authentic leadership theory. An overview of authentic leadership is first presented, before examining the framework of purpose driven leadership and the relevance and benefits of leadership purpose for the small business leader. This discussion will provide a foundation of understanding in the application of stories in finding, defining and telling leadership purpose explored in Chap. 5.

4.2 Authentic Leadership

4.2.1 Growing Interest

There are countless theories of leadership. For over half a century leadership scholars have studied the leadership phenomenon in an attempt to define the style, characteristics of great leaders, but to no avail. While research to date has not produced a blueprint of the ideal leader there is recognition that effective leadership can emerge from the life stories of the individual forged by a lifelong commitment to learning, classified as Authentic Leadership (George 2003). There is no doubt that profound changes in society and economic and political instability has also fuelled growing interest in authentic leadership. For instance, fatal terrorist attacks in public spaces and public failures by well-known institutions and banks, not to mention atypical appointments in the political arena, has created unprecedented uncertainty.

Moreover, new challenges, technologies, market demands, and evolving competition on global scale are challenging business organisations of all shapes and sizes throughout the world. In the words of Robin Sharma, what used to work doesn't always work anymore. People have developed a deep mistrust of leaders, which has fuelled the focus on what constitutes genuine leadership by scholars and practitioners (George 2007). This research at Harvard underlines the need for a new kind of business leader. That is, authentic leaders with purpose, values and integrity that builds enduring organisations and creates long-term value for shareholders and/or stakeholders.

4.2.2 Defining Authentic Leadership

Authentic leadership represents one of the newest areas of leadership research drawing upon fields of leadership, organisational scholarship and ethics (Northouse 2013).

Distinct models of authentic leadership have been developed (see for example Gardner 1995; Luthans and Avolio 2003) and provide understanding of the components, influencing factors, and the characteristics of authentic leadership. For instance, literature review and interview research by Walumba and associates in (2008) identified four components of authentic leadership: self-awareness, internalised moral perspective, balanced processing, and relational transparency. Moreover, Luthans and Avolio (2003) build on positive psychology and positive organisational behaviour to define the key influencing factors of authentic leadership as confidence, hope, optimism and resilience. But, at the core of authentic leadership is the relationship between the leader and followers, which is co-dependent on the authentication of the leader by the follower (Shamir and Eilam 2005). The co-dependency aspect of authentic leadership on employee followership can reap positive impact on creativity and innovation in the business (Müceldili et al. 2013).

4.2.3 Clarifying Authentic Leadership

In terms of the characteristics of authentic leaders, the seminal work of Bill George (2003, 2007) interviewed 125 leaders to explore the development of leadership abilities. They found authentic leadership is defined by a clear and unique expression by the leader who is true to themselves, motivated by a larger purpose and not ego, demonstrated by high integrity and by sound decisions made independent of profit or political expediency, and results driven in a way that creates sustained value. Defining the key dimensions relates not to the leadership style of the individual, but rather five characteristics of purpose, strong values, trusting relationships, self-discipline, and acting from the heart. This is echoed in a later study by Shamir and Eilam (2005) who on a similar found note authentic leaders do not fake their leadership, lead from conviction, are originals not copies, and their actions are based on values and convictions of the head and heart.

Northouse (2013) explains from a practical perspective that the theoretical perspective of authentic leadership only works if leaders are committed to a lifelong process of learning influenced by critical life events and explained in story form. While many agree authenticity matters, others find it difficult to fully explain the concept and in practical terms, how to achieve it (Sinek 2011). We are constantly evaluating the words and actions of others assessing if they can be trusted, so often the reality of authentic leadership is associated with outward actions of accountability, compassion, vulnerability and transparency. So, if we consider politicians, on one hand we may believe their spoken words, but on the other we may doubt the motive of their argument (are they simply selling a vote?) But, it is the inward journey of authentic leadership that leads to the external manifestation of these characteristics, which in turn can only be validated by followers.

In reality, development is highly personal and may have to largely natural in order to be authentic (Shamir and Eilam 2005). In other words it cannot be copied from one leader to another. Ultimately, it requires a strong internal compass i.e. doing the right thing for the right reasons and in the right way (George 2003). However, there is no doubt that dealing with the challenges of maintaining authenticity requires an inner strength and energy by the leader to persist in face of obstacles.

4.2.4 The Debate

The body of authentic leadership knowledge is arguably still in the formative phase of development (Northouse 2013). While most people agree we would rather follow a leader who is for real, rather than someone who is faking it, not all view the rise of authentic leadership in a positive way (Gruenfeld and Zander 2011). The concept that "being true to yourself" will make you a better leader can also be perceived as a negative characteristic. A very recent case in point is the success of the new USA President Donald Trump and his frank talking leadership style. As Hill (2017) argues, Mr Trump could turn out to be a number of versions of the "authentic leader", and not all of them palatable, and indeed, some may even argue he is not authentic at all. This underlines our predisposition of dislike towards lone ranger leaders and how we rather seek out connection, community and leaders with courage to follow.

According to some, authenticity, through abuse and overuse, is well on its way to becoming a management cliché (Hill 2017). In their much-cited article in Harvard Business Review in 2011, Deborah Gruenfeld and Lauren Zander argue in practice, sometimes placing value on being authentic has become an excuse for bad behavior.

In some cases in business, hiding behind the authenticity excuse is a convenient way of avoiding the truth about who we really are, how we actually behave, and why (Gruenfeld and Zander 2011). They argue that it is important to realise that for most people, what comes naturally can also get pretty nasty- in fact, it is often these most authentic parts of a leader that need the most management (Gruenfeld and Zander 2011). Therefore, to counter the harmful side of authentic leadership, there is need to understand the fuller vision of human nature, founded in genetics, psychology and neurosciences shaped through life experiences and how leaders express it through decisions and behaviour (Kiel 2015). To be sure, it is the voices of significant others i.e. the followers, that not only validates the authenticity of the leader, but their feedback will also generate greater self-awareness if accepted by the leader.

4.3 Leading with Purpose

4.3.1 Roots of Purpose

The notion of 'purpose' is not a new one. Indeed, there is a vast body of literature that refers to the importance of individual and personal purpose. In the broadest sense of the term, purpose springs from identity; in many cases externally presented as a distinctive personal brand. According to Inam (2015) it shows up in the unique talents we have and we use to contribute to a better world and however it shows up, when we find it or it finds us, we come alive. Russell and Underwood (2016) conducted a review of literature and found little attention has been given specifically to purpose in leadership (a total of two peer-reviewed papers). As previously discussed, authentic leaders know their purpose, but purpose is not only recognised in authentic leadership theory. It is also rooted in theoretical models such as ethical leadership (Brown et al. 2005) and values-based leadership (Frost 2014). However, as Russell and Underwood (2016) explain, these approaches are in essence 'style' theories, defining static leadership characteristics required for success (van Knippenberg and Sitkin 2013).

4.3.2 The 'What' and 'Why' of Leadership Purpose

Recent research by Russell and Underwood (2016) defines the 'what' of leadership purpose as:

> A leader who defines success in terms of the legacy they will leave, the impact they intend to make in achieving both financial and business objectives, and more widely in terms of impact at the team, organisational and stakeholder level. A leader with purpose is concerned to align their own personal values with their definition of success, and achieve a sense of meaning and wellbeing in attaining their goals.

In global business terms, the 'why' of purpose is clearly articulated by Craig and Snooks (2014) who argue it is the key to navigating the complex volatile and ambiguous world today, where strategy is ever changing and few decisions are obviously right or wrong. Based on research with global business organisations such as Heineken, GE, Unilever, and Ben and Jerrys, the Authentic Leadership Institute present evidence of the wider benefits of leadership purpose for the leader and organisation:

- Business experts say it is key to exceptional performance
- Psychologists say it is pathway to greater mental well being
- Doctors say these leaders are less prone to disease

The purpose leadership development programmes delivered by the Harvard team has helped more than 1000 leaders and witnessed dramatic results ranging from two-step promotions to sustained improvement in business results (Craig and Snooks 2014). Outside academia, there are several thought leaders on the subject of leadership purpose who similarly argue it makes better leaders and more successful organisations. For instance, Inam (2015) specifically refers to the benefits for female leaders. She points to the McKinsey's Centered Leadership project that demonstrates the correlation with a sense of meaning, which becomes a powerful motivator for women enabling greater courage and resilience.

Purpose leadership is not confined to the personal and professional skills development of the leader, but can be used to develop a shared mission for the business that engages the heart and mind of others. This is echoed in Simon Sinek's biological perspective of leadership that demonstrates how great leaders inspire action through a contagious sense of purpose. In a similar way, drawing upon the positive psychology discipline, Steenberger (2015) refers to mission-based leadership, which defines the engagement with followers as elicit perspiration through inspiration, underpinned with the sense of 'we are doing something important'. In this way, Steenberger (2015) argues leadership purpose is not just a set of qualities that we have, but rather the why is a process for cultivating the best in others by consistently tapping into missions that capture our own deepest values and strengths.

4.3.3 Integration of Purpose

Finding purpose and the courage to live it is the most important developmental task as a leader will undertake (Craig and Snooks 2014). At the core of developing a model of purpose driven leadership, is the integration of the leader's inner and outer journey of purpose.

The character based leadership research by Kiel (2015) revisits the traditional understanding of leadership based on self-interest and celebrates the meaningful connection between who we are and what we do i.e. purpose. The inner journey is the development of self-awareness marked 'not by what you do, but how you do your job and why- the strengths and passions you bring to the table no matter where you are seated' (Craig and Snooks 2014, 5). For the leader, it is about self-understanding through reflection in forming a worldview (mental model of reality and catalogue system for arranging beliefs about external world and events, formed from life experiencing, culture or social group, mentors, friends) to develop the mental complexity necessary to empower continuous improvement (Kiel 2015). But, this commands courage. The outward journey on the other hand, is presented by the critical relationships with parents, family, teachers, mentors, employers, colleagues and other influential adults spanning personal and professional contexts.

Ultimately, the goal of purpose driven leadership is not one of either pursuing the inner or outer journey of the leader, but rather it should adopt a holistic view of work and family. To lead with purpose is to lead with balance. In order to do so, it requires the leader to bring together all the constituent elements of life encompassing work, family, community and friends. As Bill George and his colleagues explain "you are the same person in each environment … (so) think of your life as a house, with a bedroom for your personal life, a study for your professional life, a family room with your family and a living room to share with friends" (George 2003, 7). In many ways, this alludes to Kiel's 'Integrated Human' leader who is self-aware and committed to self-improvement, thereby in turn creating the most value for their organisations through both increased levels of workforce engagement and stronger financial returns (Kiel 2015).

The leadership purpose model developed by Russell and Underwood (2016) asserts that a sense of purpose is created throughout life's journey and encapsulates one's personal values, goals and identity. In many ways, this model illustrates not only the characteristics of those who lead with purpose and those who do not, but also what drives behaviour, how success is defined and how this success is achieved. While a sense of purpose, not a specific set of characteristics, is the key to successful leadership for business, it is found that personal characteristics, as well as timing and context can act as barriers or facilitators to purpose (Russell and Underwood 2016). The model by Russell and Underwood (2016) also contends that key internal facilitators are mainly concerned with the leader's style (their behaviours, thought processes and emotions), but this is only as a moderator of success rather than as a direct predictor of it. As such, leaders with purpose define success as more than business and financial objectives—for example leaving a legacy. But, this sense of purpose is often time-bound and personal to each leader, something that individuals often understand, but organisations may not. The primary implications of this model are to aid business owners and managers in the selection processes to better identify strong leadership potential, as well as in leadership development programmes with a foundation for individual coaching.

Chapter 5 discusses in more detail how to find and define purpose through stories, but the leadership purpose model by Craig and Snooks (2014) tells us in the first instance purpose is discovered by identifying core, lifelong strengths, values, and passions in the leader's inner life story. Akin to the Russell and Underwood (2016) model of leadership purpose, the meaning of purpose most often stems from having overcome significant challenges or being influenced by significant others in their life and career. As part of this process, the leader must explore crucible moments; defined as transformational events born out of difficulty yet enabling the reframing of events to discover their passion to lead (George 2007). These events show the real plot in the leader's story. It could be a new job or assignment, significant reversal in professional or personal life, or a protracted challenge or opportunity that goes on for a long time.

The second part of this leadership development journey then finds the unifying thread throughout the inner journey that uncovers the purpose statement of the leader. The next chapter gives more detail on how to find and define purpose, but practically, it is an important aspect of your personal brand and leadership impact (Inam 2015). Proactively articulating our personal brand helps the business leader be more inspired and accountable for their leadership impact. But, it is critically important that leaders link their defined purpose with the mission and role played in the organisation (Inam 2015). The implications for small business leaders are specifically explored in the following and final section of this chapter.

4.4 Significance for Small Business

Purpose requires confidence by the leader, underpinned by the conviction of the small business leader to make it happen (Young 2013). While purpose should be innate and natural for small businesses it requires confidence on behalf of the leader to mobilise for impact. Given that the owner's experiences, skills and competencies are key influencers on business survival and growth (Kelliher and Reinl 2009), the significance of purpose is relevant for several key reasons:

1. Underlines the important correlation between purpose and action to growing the business (often small firms fail by spreading the organisation too thinly by trying to be all things to all people)
2. Addresses market failure in small firms who often lack a strong sense of their leadership purpose (thereby failing to achieve their most ambitious professional and personal goals)
3. Recognises the high person-role merger by adopting a holistic view of the professional and personal lives of the small business leader (where these two lives are one)
4. Realises the significant influence of family, outside interests and commitments on leader decision-making (that can serve as positive and negative factors in forming and mobilising purpose)

4.4.1 Purpose and Profits

The business landscape has becomes more nuanced than ever with the rise of small socially aware enterprises who operate on a mission of profit with purpose. Take for instance the success of small global companies such as TOMS who trade with an altruistic purpose operating a one-for-one model- whenever you buy a pair of TOMS shoes, it will donate a pair to a child in need. As explained by Besley and Ghatak (2017) there is much interest today in more flexible organisational forms, which combine profit with purpose. Taking into account the growing importance of leadership purpose for businesses in yielding real impact, it may be argued that the traditional distinction between for-profit and non-profit organisations it less clear than it was. Indeed, the fact over half of the Millennial generation is already in leadership positions, is shaping new leader behaviours that is impacting upon the meaning of doing business. This new wave of leadership, which thrives on recognition and not just financial rewards, is placing a greater emphasis on purpose and mission.

Many bigger corporates realise the business value of purpose, which is most often presented as corporate social responsibility or as the values of the business. Research evidence published by the CMI indicates that "value" can represent the social value of a product or service provided by either the profit or not-for-profit sector, and not just financial returns within the private sector. The report suggests that the best organisations have a purpose that serves others and strong values that inform better decisions, which demonstrates that while financial results are essential for accountability, this is only one part of the story when it comes to measuring performance (CMI 2014). This work goes on to point out smaller companies and social enterprises have a clear purpose from the start, therefore for these firms, purpose is something innate and theoretically should be easier to define for the leader of the business (Pereira 2015).

4.4.2 Purpose and People

The foundation of greatness is usually laid while the company is still small and malleable enough to be handcrafted into an entity that fully embodies the values of its leaders (Collins 2001). According to Collins and Lazier (1992) IBM is great because of things Tom Watson did long before IBM became the monolith that it is today and NIKE is great because of things Phil Knight did when NIKE was a scrappy David taking on Goliaths. It is the small business leader who is the architect of greatness (Collins 2001). But, as small firms, the leaders must find the motivation to lead and the energy to persist in the face of obstacles and setbacks, operating from strong convictions and high level of purpose in order to grow the business. The reality of working in small business organisations cannot be viewed through rose tinted spectacles—it can be challenging managing limited resources in highly competitive markets (as outlined in Chap. 2 and the stories told in Chaps. 7 and 8). But, the evidence pointing out the benefits to small business is strong; it tells us that engagement is higher when staff believe they are doing something worthwhile (Pereira 2015).

The integration of people and purpose for the small business is an enedavour that Steenberger (2015) refers to as cultivating the best in others by consistently tapping into missions that capture our own deepest values and strengths. According to research this requires the leader to fight "short termism" and develop a long-term strategy that shies away from "quick fixes" such as brutal cost-cutting strategies and large-scale redundancy programmes unless they are absolutely necessary (CMI 2014). In doing so, it is recommended that successful long-term leadership should review and focus on three critical areas: how they define their purpose, how they lead and develop their people, and how they invest in their potential. But, while purpose is arguably innate in small business and can be defined by the leader for the business mission, the engagement with staff is weak across the UK. The study by CMI (2014) found only 36% of small organisations (one to 50 employees) say they define and publish their commitment to their employees, compared to 58% of large organisations (over 1000 employees).

4.4.3 Mobilising Purpose

Small businesses generally start local, and some grow to serve larger markets. But it's not necessarily important to get to larger markets if being small fits a business's purpose (Brown 2016). Research conducted in the

UK has found examples of small firms who have achieved high growth in mobilising their purpose (CMI 2014). The benefits are not only found in growing market share, but engagement with staff and customers. In the case of Belu (a clear green water company in the UK focused on ethical and environmental issues), they have found "people find it easier to engage in brands that are trying to do something positive; when they stop and think about a business and 'get it', loyalty builds very quickly. The challenge is to get people to stop in the first place" (Pereira 2015, 55).

These types of small firms with a strong social purpose underpinning business are very attractive to the Millennial generation (otherwise defined as Generation Y) who look for ethical employers and interesting work. A job is more than just that to Generation Y. The managers who belong to this generation want to work somewhere where there is a positive, values-driven culture (CMI 2014). In this report, the top ten characteristics of highly effective leaders in 2020 are presented at number one is a clear sense of purpose. It is argued that employees need to understand what their leaders are trying to do, why they are trying to do it, and what it will achieve not only for the organisation itself but for the wider community and society (CMI 2014).

The research by CMI also describes the greatest challenges for small business leaders in realising the benefits as twofold. The first challenge is mobilising purpose and putting it to action in the business. This requires time for reflection and strategy, which comes at a premium cost to the leader. While purpose will guide the leader of the small business, it's passion that propels the business forward (Brown 2016). Secondly, an additional challenge for the leader is avoiding the temptation to extend and expand the mission. There is always a temptation to over diversify in responding to commercial opportunities to reach a wide customer base. Most small businesses struggle with this. Yet, this endeavor only serves to dilute the message and clutters the business model making it more difficult to manage the supply chain and market to an increasingly diverse customer base. In this way, sometimes the purpose of a business can get confused. By its very nature, the evidence from CMI (2015) insists a purpose-driven organisation will exclude itself from certain opportunities, but a focused leader in staying true north will see a net gain of product and service quality and success (Pereira 2015).

4.5 Chapter Summary

This chapter has presented the 'what' and 'how' of leadership purpose and with strong and undisputed evidence from UK and USA, and the case is strong. Yet, few organisations and their leaders know their purpose and how to put it to work, thereby failing to achieve goals (Craig and Snooks 2014). There is an opportunity for small business leaders to articulate their purpose and put it to work with greater ease and less effort than larger corporations. For two reasons: first, most often a new business is formed from a passion or interest or desire to solve a problem. Secondly, the simple and flatter organisational structure in theory should enable direct communication and direct impact with a greater chance of employee commitment.

References

Besley, T., and M. Ghatak. 2017. Profit with purpose? A theory of social enterprise. *American Economic Journal: Economic Policy*.

Bresin, J. 2013. Millennials will soon rule the world: But how will they lead? *Forbes*, 13 September.

Brown, B. 2016. *Daring greatly: How the courage to be vulnerable transforms the way we live, love, parent, and lead*. New York: Avery Publishing Group.

Brown, M.E., Treviño, L.K. and Harrison, D.A., 2005. Ethical leadership: A social learning perspective for construct development and testing. *Organizational behavior and human decision processes* 97 (2): 117–134.

CMI. 2014. Management 2020 Report: Leadership to unlock long-term growth, The commission on the future of Leadership and Management, July 2014.

CMI 2015. Growing your small business: The role of business schools and professional bodies. Chartered Management Institute Publication, September.

Collins, J. 2001. Good to great. Why some companies make the leap and others don't. Harper Business, United States of America.

Collins, J., and W. Lazier. 1992. *Beyond entrepreneurship: Turning your business into an enduring great company*. Upper Saddle River, NY: Prentice Hall Direct.

Craig, N. and Snooks, S. 2014. From Purpose to Impact: Figure Out Your Passion and Put It to Work. *Harvard Business Review* 92 (5): 105–111.

Frost, D. (ed.). 2014. *Transforming education through teacher leadership.* Cambridge: LfL.

Gardner. 1995. *Leading minds: An anatomy of leadership.* New York: Basic Books.

George, B. 2003. *Authentic leadership: Rediscovering the secrets to creating lasting value.* San Francisco: Wiley Publishing House.

George, W. 2007. *True north: Discover your authentic leadership.* San Francisco: Jossey-Bass.

Gruenfeld, D., and L. Zander. 2011. Authentic leadership can be bad leadership, *Harvard Business Review*, 3 February.

Hill, A. 2017. Trump's plain speaking fuels the leadership cult of authenticity. *Financial Times*, February 6. Online available at: https://www.ft.com/content/f168807e-e8a8-11e6-893c-082c54a7f539.

Inam, H. 2015. *Wired for authenticity: Seven practices to inspire, adapt and lead.* Bloomington: iUniverse.

Kelliher, F., and L. Reinl. 2009. A resource-based view of micro-firm management practice. *Journal of Small Business and Enterprise Development* 16 (3): 521–532.

Kiel, F. 2015. *Return on character: The Real reason leaders and their companies win.* Boston, MA: Harvard Business Review Press.

Luthans, F., and B.J. Avolio. 2003. Authentic leadership: A positive development approach. In *Positive organizational scholarship: Foundations of a new discipline*, ed. K.S. Cameron, J.E. Dutton, and R.E. Quinn, 241–261. San Francisco: Berrett-Koehler.

Müceldili, B., H. Turan, and O. Erdil. 2013. The influence of authentic leadership on creativity and innovativeness. *Social and Behavioural Sciences* 99 (65): 673–681.

Northouse, P.G. 2013. *Leadership: Theory and practice*, 6th ed. Chicago: Thousand Oaks.

Pereira. 2015. The heart of small business. Professional manager, Chartered Management Institute, Winter 2015, pp. 53–55.

Russell, E., and C. Underwood. 2016. Exploring the role of purpose. *HR Magazine*, June 1.

Shamir, B., and G. Eilam. 2005. What's your story? A life-stories approach to authentic leadership development. *The Leadership Quarterly* 16(3): 395–417.

Shamir, B., D. Dayan-Horesh, and D. Adler. 2005. Leading by biography: Towards a life story approach to the study of leadership. *Leadership* 1 (1): 13–29.

Sinek, S. 2011. *Start With Why: How Great Leaders Inspire Everyone To Take Action*. Penguin: USA

Steenbarger, B. 2015. Mission-based management: The leadership of purpose. *Forbes*, 19 July.

van Knippenberg, D., and S.B. Sitkin. 2013. A critical assessment of charismatic—Transformational leadership research: Back to the drawing board? *The Academy Of Management Annals* 7 (1): 1–60.

Walumbwa, F.O., B.J. Avolio, W.L. Gardner, T.S. Wernsing, and S.J. Peterson. 2008. Authentic leadership: Development and validation of a theory-based measure? *Journal of Management* 34: 89.

Young, Lord. 2013. *Growing your business: A report on micro firms*, May 2013. BIS/13/729, Crown copyright.

5

Stories and Storytelling for Small Business Leaders

Abstract Hutchinson unpacks the sense-making capability of stories and storytelling in the context of leading small business. Focusing on the growing importance of stories, this chapter provides leadership context to this global phenomenon for small firms. While storytelling to date has found a more lukewarm reception in business school education, this discussion demonstrates the power of stories and storytelling in assisting small business owners to find and define leadership purpose as well as communicating with employees, customers, partners, investors or other stakeholders.

Keywords Small business · Leadership · Power of stories · Storytelling Metaphor · Life stories · Narrative · Communication

5.1 Growing Importance

5.1.1 Once upon a Time….

Since the beginning of time, stories were told and shared in community. Men, women and children sitting around a fire listening to each others stories is a common image signifying social connection and identity indicative of times gone by. Stories continue to be told with the purpose to share knowledge, lessons learned, ideas, and while factual in content; it is the emotion evoked that forms the connection and lasting memory with listeners. The imagery of families and communities sitting around a fire sharing stories may no longer reflect society today, but the global phenomenon of TED Talks demonstrates how telling stories still has vitality and a sustaining presence today. Stories inform, illuminate, inspire, and can take many forms, from old-fashioned words on a page to movies laden with digital special effects (Guber 2007). Technology may have provided new ways of recording, presenting, and disseminating stories, but it isn't special effects that matter most, it's the 'oohs' and 'aahs' that the storyteller evokes from an audience (Guber 2007).

In a similar way, the stories of outstanding leaders have captivated us for years. We are drawn to them, seeking some sense of clarity as to why and how these individuals came to be the forces they did (Ligon et al. 2008). There are both practical and pedagogical reasons. According to Gardner (1995, 9) "leaders achieve their effectiveness chiefly though the stories they relate" and argues storytelling is the single most powerful weapon in the leader's literary arsenal. Storytelling is a phenomenon fundamental to nations, societies and culture (Denning 2005). Whether, politician, entrepreneur, or chief executive, leaders tell different types of stories with great frequency and for many different purposes such as influencing, persuading, illustrating or projecting a desired image. Stories help make sense of a rapidly morphing global economy, and the most powerful are those that draw upon personal, autobiographical experience (McAdams 2014). Why? It is argued life stories validate a leader's authenticity (Shamir and Eilam 2005).

5.1.2 Art or Science?

Stories are "data with soul" and a powerful and versatile form of human communication (Bruner 1990). The inherent power of telling a story is manifest when the communication reaches minds and touches hearts. Forman (2013) tells us that professional storytellers express our intuitive understanding that *'people are hardwired for stories'*. She explains that the familiar beginning and ending of fairy tales starting with 'once upon a time…. and they lived happily ever after' act as verbal bookends, depicting how things work, or ought to be. The gifted storyteller not only compels attention, but also creates an intimate link between the listener and the teller of the tale. Simply put, the storyteller orchestrates it all.

There is also science behind the power of storytelling. According to Schwertly (2015), in reacting to data or facts, only two parts of the brain engage i.e. language comprehension and language processing. So, by sharing facts and statistics with an audience, the response to the presenter is either agreement or disagreement. But, rather tell a story and seven areas of the brain engage including the visual cortex (colours and shapes), the olfactory cortex (scents), the auditory cortex (sounds), the motor cortex (movement), and the sensory cortex and cerebellum (language comprehension). That is five more than the simple presentation of facts! As Schwertly (2015) explains, this is testament to why as humans we love stories. Stories don't spark agreement or disagreement but rather participation. They trigger emotional responses that are memorable. In the world of business, to tell a story (well), is the most efficient way for business leaders to ignite the brain of employees, and connect with the values of customers or shareholders.

5.1.3 Changing Narrative

In a time of extraordinary change, the nature of stories has changed. While, the power of stories remains unaffected, Neumeier (2008) argues that when it comes to marketing, we now live in a world of participatory theatre. He believes customers are not focused on products, but meaning. In other words, they choose products to build their identities. They are no longer content to sit in the audience and be *told* the story, but rather they want to *tell* the story. The changing narrative of stories has led to the development of new framework away from 'Story telling' to 'Story framing', whereby he explains "the discipline of building a structure that lets customers create their own narratives" (Neumeier 2008, 116), while ensuring that boundaries keep the story contained. In the same way, Forman (2013) refers to the voices of significant others and how the growing presence of social network technology enables employees and external stakeholders (e.g. investors, customers, clients) want to be heard and at same time have their stories told in their own voices.

A traditional view of leadership depicts a top-down process of influence, often characterised by dictatorial and charismatic approach in leading people. Whereas recent thought leadership emphasises the importance and relevance of distributed or team based leadership that influences by co-creating a sense of belonging and connection with followers. Today, employees or customers don't want to be broadcast to or lectured to, but rather they seek interaction and engagement. Stories told by the leader of the business can help build, express, strengthen and celebrate corporate culture with employees and customers, or indeed any stakeholder (Forman 2013), but it is important that he or she develops the narrative of the story by carefully listening to the audience. As research by Forman (2013) found, "CEOs who know about storytelling and strategy will bring people along. Storytelling allows you to connect with people and allows them to participate in the story as characters" (Forman 2013, 53).

5.2 Business Context

5.2.1 Multidisciplinary Validation

Advocacy for storytelling comes from a variety of disciplines and a wide range of professions including neurologists, physicians, economists, lawyers, historians, filmmakers, and cognitive psychologists (Forman 2013). This multidisciplinary practice of storytelling reveals a wealth of benefits, from making sense of experiences to reaching audiences emotionally, as well as wielding explanatory and persuasive powers.

Yet, notwithstanding endorsement across industries, storytelling is valued less in business than other professions, and as a result has generally found a lukewarm reception in business school education (Forman 2013). The reasons for this are varied, but ultimately prevalent misconceptions in the world of business are to blame.

There are three common misunderstandings. First, there is a general perception that stories are child's play whereas business is all about numbers and models. Hence, stories can be perceived to be at odds with data and theory of which both dominate business education programmes. This has resulted in an anti-story bias in business where there tends to be an overreliance on charts, graphs, tables and power point bullet points. Second, many believe the purpose of stories is to entertain. However, as Guber (2007) explains, the use of the story is not only to delight, but also to instruct and lead the audience. Third, some perceive storytelling conflicts with authenticity in that the storyteller is a spinner of yarns with very little essence of truth (Guber 2007). Yet, effective storytelling in business is fostered on the integrity of the story and its teller and can be one of the world's most powerful tools for achieving astonishing results (Guber 2007). As the recent research by Forman (2013) demonstrates, the case for stories and storytelling in business may be muted but is most significant.

5.2.2 Metaphor as Story

Chapter 2 introduced the concept of metaphor and told the story of small business by using the metaphor of plant biology. Academics in the field of entrepreneurship point to the work of cognitive scientists in proposing life narratives offer access to the most fundamental and important form of human cognition- that of understanding our lives and ourselves (Cardon et al. 2005). As such it is argued a research methodology, which examines the use of metaphors in the life narratives of entrepreneurs, could be expected to yield results which "interest, inform, provoke" (Aldrich 1992, p. 38). The study of US entrepreneurs by Cardon et al. (2005) used the methodology of harvesting and analysing metaphors to give meaning to their life-and-business stories. As will be explained later in this chapter, leaders in reviewing their life story, often found a dramatic metaphor to describe their leadership purpose and tell their story contextualised in their specific business/personal circumstances to engage the hearts, minds and motivations of their staff and/or customer. This metaphor is embodied within a purpose statement for instance using imagery from phrases such as "the grit in the oyster" to "wuxia master" (Craig and Snooks 2014).

The role of story and metaphor is applied in business novels through the use of fables to advocate a particular approach to organisational change management (e.g. Kotter and Rathgeber 2006). Moreover, it can also be used as a way to interpret and manage organisational change differently (Reissner et al. 2011). On one hand, the use of story can help managers communicate more effectively, spark action (Denning 2005), and engage organisational actors in change (Armstrong 1992). Metaphor, in contrast, 'carries over' meaning from one domain to another (Morgan 1997) and can open up new ways of thinking and acting (Barrett and Cooperrider 1990; Broussine and Vince 1996). Argued by Reissner et al. (2011), brought together, story and metaphor can enhance communication about organisational change and its management, as evident in Kotter and Rathgeber's well-known and well-read fable of change management "Our Iceberg is melting", which is a powerful message about the fear of change and how to motivate people to face the future and take action. Therefore, in the context of this book in understanding small business leadership and purpose through the power of storytelling, there is no doubt as to the relevance and significance of metaphorical expression to engage the reader in deeper understanding and engagement.

5.2.3 Business Case

The business benefits of stories and storytelling have been researched over recent years by various authors, encompassing aspects of business organisations such as leadership, strategy, culture, and brand communication. As someone once said, ideas that catch on are wrapped in a story. Essentially, stories construct shared meanings that serve to provide the rationale by which the past, present, and future of the business comes together (Boal and Schultz 2007). This sense-making capability has both a practical and action oriented purpose. The purpose may be to gain or consolidate the trust of the audience, and with this achieved, inform, persuade and inspire them (Forman 2013). Alternatively, it can be adopted to achieve specific business objectives such as recruiting a new member of staff, increasing customer base, or building a corporate brand. In this way, stories become a force for turning dreams into goals and goals into results (Guber 2007), creating sustained and significant impact on business growth and sustainability.

We live and work in a highly pressurised environment: "we multitask, we text-message, we surf the Web, we tweet and we check Facebook in settings, virtual or real" (Forman 2013, 3). Thus, much business communication takes the form of instantaneous sound bites and shorthand thinking. Yet Forman (2013) tells us despite this, a well-chosen, well-crafted story can get through to people. Her research found a story can build a narrative for topics that go deeper and live longer in a person's psyche than other forms of communication. One way of creating connection with customers or employees is to start telling the story from the very beginning i.e. focus on the "once upon a time". For large global organisations, the 'once upon a time' is an important story to tell. Take for instance, Larry Page and Sergey Brin who established Google or Jeff Bezos the founder of Amazon, and indeed much further back in time when Walt Roy Disney started the Disney Brothers Cartoon Studio. These examples clearly illustrate how the big almost always starts in the small for these successful businesses, with important lessons for wannabe entrepreneurs and the owners of small businesses who have the vision for growth and success but are struggling to make ends meet.

5.3 Leadership Purpose

5.3.1 The 'Story' of Leadership Purpose

Chapter 4 presented a discussion on the theoretical framework of purpose driven leadership derived from the authentic leadership school of

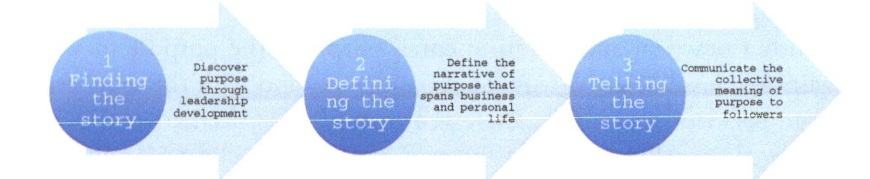

Fig. 5.1 The 'story' of leadership purpose. *Source* Authors own

thought. Taking on board the argument that leaders find and define their purpose by understanding and writing their story (George 2003, 2007), recent research by Hutchinson (as presented in this book) with small business owners, shines the light on a third critical stage of leadership purpose process: telling the story. The overall three stage process of the leadership purpose journey is illustrated in Fig. 5.1.

Figure 5.1 illustrates for small business leaders the story of leadership purpose and reflects how "we live life forward, but understand it backwards" (Shamir et al. 2005, 17). In the first stage, revisiting life stories can help the small business owner leader discover purpose by identifying core, lifelong strengths, values, and passions in their life stories (Craig and Snooks 2014). The second stage defines the narrative or 'why' of leadership purpose i.e. the unifying thread throughout the stories that uncovers the purpose statement of the leader spanning their personal and business life (Craig and Snooks 2014). Finally, the third stage is about telling the story. In other words, communicating the collective meaning of leadership purpose to influence followers, whether employees, investors, shareholders, customers. The subsequent discussion will explain each stage in more detail.

5.3.2 Finding the Story

The first stage for the small business owner is perhaps the greatest challenge of all. For the small business owner to find purpose, it requires commitment of the head and heart. Particularly, it necessitates the willingness to fully engage with an unconventional leadership development programme focused on promoting self-awareness through reflection on life stories and feedback from peers. Indeed, even if the small business owner has the will, there are additional and significant challenges in terms of committing time to this activity with resource constraints prioritising tangible operational needs over new learning, which is more intangible. Moreover, the small business owner can experience conflicting advice (whether invited or not!), as employees, customers, family, friends, and shareholders can be quick to tell the owner of the business how to lead. But, as outlined in the previous chapter, the benefits of this activity far outweigh the challenges, proving it is the most important development task a leader can undertake (George 2003, 2007; Craig and Snooks 2014; CMI Report 2014).

If leadership purpose springs from identity i.e. who the leader is, then it is argued the leader will find purpose i.e. the 'why', in their life story (George 2003, 2007; Craig and Snooks 2014). In a nutshell, when people revisit and revise their life stories they gain clarity about who they are. Life stories according to Shamir and Eilam (2005) are valuable for two primary reasons. Firstly, life stories are a source of self-knowledge and self-concept clarity, providing the leader with a meaning system and clarity about their values and convictions. Secondly, life stories as self-justification, not only 'who am I stories', but 'why I am here' stories (Simmons 2002). The high person-role merger, characteristic of authentic leaders, means the life story not only recounts, but justifies (Shamir and Eilam 2005). This could include a story of the leader that demonstrates how leadership was developed over time as a natural process, or through coping with difficulties, or as part of self-improvement through learning, or finding a cause (Shamir and Eilam 2005). This is critical given leaders are authentic to extent to which they act and justify their actions on the basis of the meaning system supplied by their life stories.

The emphasis on the leader's self-development to find purpose through the construction and revising of their life stories marks a shift away from the predominant focus of leadership development programmes on the acquisition of skills and behaviourial traits. It marks a new approach to understanding leadership development (Mumford and Manley 2003). It shows that we should be paying attention to the influence of developmental experiences and in what way they are construed in the context of leaders' lives. Uniquely, it recognises four influencing factors on leadership development, encompassing the leader's positive psychological capacities, the effect of role models, moral reasoning capacities, and critical life events or crucibles (Shamir and Eilam 2005). First, positive psychological capacities encompass confidence, hope, optimism, and resilience. Second, the effect of role models historical or public figures, parents, siblings, family members, teachers, peers, but role models not for imitation, but inspiration. Thirdly, moral reasoning capacities including decisions around right and wrong, and promoting justice, or the greater good of the organisation in the community. Finally, critical life events also known as crucibles (defining experiences that transform a person), whether positive or negative can be a catalyst for change.

The point of revisiting life stories is to identify core, lifelong strengths, values, and passions. By finding the unifying thread in the life stories, purpose becomes unveiled. But, this is more than a philosophy, but in practice yields real business benefits. So how is this achieved for the small business owner? The first task is for the leader to mine their life story for common threads and major themes that reveal lifelong passions and values (Craig and Snooks 2014). This development approach is highly personal and has to be natural in order to be authentic (Shamir and Eilam 2005). While there are limits to extent to which this can be planned and guided, it doesn't mean it can't be assisted. Research by Craig and Snooks (2014) has found a variety of prompts to help leaders in the exploration of leadership purpose as presented:

1. What did you especially love doing when you were a child, before the world told you what you should or shouldn't like or do? Describe a moment and how it made you feel.
2. Tell us about two of your most challenging life experiences. How have they shaped you?
3. What do you enjoy doing in your life now that helps you sing your song?

Research by Albert and Vadla (2009) found that students came to understand through the process of reconstructing personal experiences (historical truth) that these previous experiences had profound impact on their current reality (narrative truth). Not only did this learning invoke deeply significant questions of purpose, direction and meaning, it became an effective means of equipping students with tools to enhance their own reflective practice (Albert and Vadla 2009). This work defined the development process according to three key types of stories: who I am, who we are and future stories. Firstly, "Who am I as a leader stories" serve as foundational to values and beliefs of the individual, they include description of events, relationships, and situations important in shaping beliefs. Secondly, "Who we are leader stories" about a group, family, or organisation involves significant events and experiences that have shaped the common identity of the individual. Thirdly, "Future stories" shares a view of future goals, dreams, vision presented by a leader, which can be difficult to create, but needs to go beyond known boundaries and what we have been told.

This research underlines the importance of the learning environment that ensures a meaningful learning experience for the leaders (Albert and Vadla 2009). Critical to supporting the process of definition of purpose is first the creation of a safe place facilitated by the instructor's willingness to be vulnerable and providing the safety, support and challenge needed for the individual to explore and develop their narrative/identity. Secondly, fostering the notion of authorship that encourages individuals to become authors of their own stories and avoid imitating someone else, but connects to a current value, belief or vocation of the individual. Thirdly, the capacity and willingness of leaders to explore the unknown through trust, vulnerability and support in the group is also important (Albert and Vadla 2009). Ultimately, in constructing the life story of the leader, the focus is less about facts and more about meaning i.e. the expression of experience. This reflection involves highlighting certain parts and ignoring others, but essentially it is about constructing truth by legitimately selecting and emphasising certain events and participants in the service of this purpose (Shamir and Eilam 2005).

5.3.3 Defining the Story

The second stage in the process necessitates defining the narrative or 'why' of leadership purpose. This narrative represents the sensemaking structure of the life stories explored in the first stage of the process. As explained by Josselson (1993), this is not record of facts, of how things actually are, but a meaning-making system that makes sense out of the chaotic mass of perceptions and experiences of a life. Likewise as argued by Kiel (2015) it is the way we understand our life story that is the critical issue. In a broader context, personality and developmental psychology researchers have also focused on concept of narrative identity and refer to an internalised and evolving story of the self that explains how the person came to be and where he/she might be heading (McAdams and McLean 2013). As Brene Brown states: "who you are is as important as what you want to achieve" (Brown 2015).

The key functions of defining a narrative are described by Shamir and Eilam (2005) and include for example, the combination of cognition and emotion to understand and make sense of events that have occurred in people's lives as an explanatory structure that allows people to maintain a sense of leader personal identity (McAdams 2001). It also serves a directive function, providing life lessons in episodic form to define goals, causes, actions, and context in the present (Baumeister and Newman 1994; Pillemer 2003), for understanding and responding to new events (Pillemer 1998; Reiser et al. 1985). Moreover, it can become a vehicle for people to communicate personal understanding of their lives in reference to the current situation (Alea and Bluck 2003; Fitzgerald 1995). It can also foster identification with followers, providing a basis for common understanding which permits more automatic, intuitive social interaction between followers and leaders (Keller 2003).

This activity of making sense of life stories for the leader is a craft. It is about recognising the threads woven together and then finding the unifying or golden thread. This can take a number of forms including for example a descriptive narrative that tells a tale or a more concise purpose statement of that explains the narrative. A longer narrative description will refer to a number of major events, both positive and negative and offers a reasonable description of the positive effect those events had on the leader's personal development (Kiel 2015). This in turn, should demonstrate how the leader's principles and beliefs are reflected in their actions and decisions for the business today. For the audience, it can serve as critical point of connection and legitimacy, in that the leader is perceived as 'one of us' or 'like me' and therefore worthy of support (McAdams 2014). Ultimately, this will (or should) speak to a leader's authenticity, or the extent to which words match deeds.

On the other hand, a narrative may be presented in the form of a purpose statement that integrates the personal and business life of the leader. This does not have to be aspirational or cause-based (e.g. "Save the whales" or "Feed the hungry"), but rather capture the essence of the leader, leaving him or her emboldened and energised with a call to action (Craig and Snooks 2014). The development of a statement narrative, cannot be crafted by the leader alone, but rather must involve feedback from trusted colleagues or friends who can act as mirrors to the business owner. Whatever, the definition (shorter statement or longer narrative), for the small business owner, it is about understanding the milestones, how they are connected and where they continue to lead. In other words, the leader knows where they are going, in part because they know where they have been, which echoes Kiel (2015) who argues we are not born great leaders, but rather we become great leaders by training how to think and act accordingly. But, it doesn't stop there, it is critically important that leaders remember to link their defined purpose with the mission and role played in the organisation (Inam 2015).

5.3.4 Telling the Story

Once the leader of the business has found and defined their purpose, the third stage is about communicating the collective meaning to an audience with intention to connect and influence followers, whether employees, investors, shareholders, customers. The leader should build on their personal purpose story to develop a wider story of purpose for the whole business that establishes common priorities and shared values for employees and customers, which in turn should yield real impact for the business organisation. But, regardless of the size of organisation, the leader is required to communicate where the business is going and how it will get there. Although, the CEOs of small companies are in effect their organisation's chief communication officer, which makes storytelling unavoidable (Forman 2013). Change is constant in the world of business, and so resilience and agility in leading and managing change has become more critical than ever before. In some ways wrapping change in a story and then telling that story in a fluent and authentic manner disguises the bitter pill of change for employees and customers and helps secure buy into the process. Story telling can also reassure leaders of leaving a positive legacy for future generations.

From the previous discussion in this chapter, the 'why' of this endeavor is understood, but it is the 'how' in telling the tale that requires specific capability and skill. Therein lies the greatest challenge of all. Storytelling is a performance art (Denning 2005), but not all business owners are confident in their ability to communicate in a fluent and authentic manner to various audiences. The challenge for many business leaders is the effective communication of the story (Armstrong 1992) and the value proposition to a range of stakeholders from the customer, to the investor, employees and partners. Charisma is not essential, but in order to do this effectively, the leader needs to develop individual and collective learning competencies built on the 'telling of stories' on purpose and with a specific mission in mind.

It is argued today that people make decisions based on emotions, then look for the facts that support their decision (Guber 2007). Therefore, the business leader's competence in the craft of storytelling centres on the ability to engage the emotions and intellect (or heart and mind) of the audience. Teaching storytelling from a communication perspective can often bring to mind lessons in presentation skills (Albert and Vadla 2009). While, there is no specific formula or blueprint, it involves significant preparation and making good choices about a variety of story elements. Forman (2013) refers to five elements of preparation essential to crafting the story: understand what needs to be achieved in story form, know the audience, choose the moment, select the right storyteller, and the characters who should be in the story.

Research by Forman (2013) developed a framework for organisational storytelling based on best practice from case study research. It is argued that the characteristics of storytelling should be authentic (credible, realistic, tangible and truthful) and fluent (engage emotions and intellect of the audience). This will include aspects of novelty and the unexpected (i.e. the incongruous juxtaposition of unlikely qualities or the subversion of a stereotype), significant details, compelling language and visuals that evoke the five senses, narrative logic, and use of technology (Forman 2013). Vulnerability in sharing a crucible story, the lessons learned, and how it forms narrative brings emotional connection to the audience in a powerful way. But, vulnerability is a challenge for many leaders, managers, salespeople, and entrepreneurs (Guber 2007). However, by willingly exposing anxieties, fears, and shortcomings, the storyteller allows the audience to identify with her and therefore brings listeners to a place of understanding and catharsis, and ultimately spurs action. Also important to effective storytelling is authenticity of the story and the storyteller is paramount, i.e. "words must match deeds" (Forman 2013).

On a practical level, there are ten principles for telling the right story, at the right time, and telling it right according to Guber (2007):

- Select the right story for the right audience: listening to the needs and wants of the audience is more important than being interesting.
- Choose when the listener will be receptive: find the place and time when the audience is least subject to interruption or distraction.
- Find the source material for good stories: most effective story comes from first hand experiences, so stockpile potential metaphors and fragments.
- Make sure the call to action resonates: this may mean finding a hero or villain in the story, showing real passion and emotion.
- Get in the right state for telling the story: this is a mental, emotional and physical process and requires a clear intention to succeed.
- Tell the story with authentic contagious energy: don't tell a story that you don't believe in—the audience will sense immediately.
- Demonstrate vulnerability and perseverance: be willing to share a fear or anxiety to strike a common denominator with the audience.
- Make the story interactive: ask for input or a response during the story to enable participation in the story.
- Engage the senses of the audience: words only account for the smallest part of human communication; the majority is non-verbal (more than half on what people see and a third transmitted through tone of voice).
- Listen actively with all senses: take time to gauge emotions, attention and interest of the audience.

From a practical and theoretical perspective, it is clear that storytelling by business leaders is not for the owner of the business to use classic mythology and adopt the hero persona, thereby creating a distance or disconnect from their audience. But, rather to use stories developed around their purpose and the business to connect and bring change for growth and improved performance.

5.4 Chapter Summary

Small business leaders must possess many skills, not only in setting strategic direction and organising complex tasks, but the ability to identify the social and interpersonal needs of the group, and then take steps to make certain their followers are satisfied. In a business environment where distractions and lack of trust dominate, stories can cut through the busyness to capture attention, engage and influence people, create meaning, exemplify values, and gain trust (Forman 2013). This chapter has presented the business benefits of stories and storytelling for leaders, with specific discussion around finding, defining and telling the story of leadership purpose for small firms. In short, the leadership purpose of the founder must align to the purpose of the business (as the two worlds are often one). From purpose the story is formed, which should be clearly and effectively communicated to attract and retain the right team for the business as well as grow a loyal customer base that will ensure sustainability of the organisation.

References

Albert, J.F., and K. Vadla. 2009. Authentic leadership development in the classroom: A narrative approach. *Journal of Leadership Education* 8 (1): 72–92.

Alea, N., and S. Bluck. 2003. Why are you telling us that? A conceptual model of the social function of autobiographical memory. *Memory* 11: 165–178.

Aldrich, H.E. 1992. Incommensurable paradigms? Vital signs from three perspectives. In *Rethinking organization: New directions in organization theory and analysis*, ed. M. Reed and M. Hughes. London: Sage.

Armstrong, David M. 1992. *Managing by storying around*. New York, NY: Doubleday.

Barrett, F.J., and D.L. Cooperrider. 1990. Generative metaphor intervention: A new approach for working with systems divided by conflict and caught in defensive perception. *Journal of Applied Behavioral Science* 26: 219–239.

Baumeister, R.F., and L.S. Newman. 1994. How stories make sense of personal experiences: Motives that shape autobiographical narratives. *Personality and Social Psychology Bulletin* 20: 676–690.

Boal, K.B., and P.L. Schultz. 2007. Storytelling, time, and evolution: The role of strategic leadership in complex adaptive systems. *The Leadership Quarterly* 18: 411–428.

Brown, B. 2015. *Daring greatly: How the courage to be vulnerable transforms the way we live, love, parent, and lead*. New York: Avery Publishing Group.

Broussine, M., and R. Vince. 1996. Working with metaphor towards organizational change. In *Organisation development: Metaphorical explorations*, ed. C. Oswick and D. Grant, 57–70. London: Pitman.

Bruner, J. 1990. *Acts of meaning*. Cambridge, MA: Harvard University Press.

Cardon, M.S., C. Zietsma, P. Saparito, B.P. Matherne, and C. Davis. 2005. A tale of passion: New insights into entrepreneurship from a parenthood metaphor. *Journal of Business Venturing* 20: 23–45.

CMI. 2014. Management 2020 report: Leadership to unlock long-term growth. The Commission on the future of Leadership and Management, July 2014.

Craig, and Snooks. 2014. Purpose to impact. *Harvard Business Review*.

Denning, S. 2005. The leader's guide to storytelling: Mastering the art and discipline of business narrative. Hoboken, NJ: Wiley.

Fitzgerald, J.M. 1995. Intensive meanings of reminiscence in adult development and aging. In *Remembering our past*, ed. D.C. Rubin, 360–393. Cambridge: Cambridge University Press.

Forman, J. 2013. *Storytelling in business: The authentic and fluent organisation*. Stanford, CA: Stanford Business Books.

Gardner, 1995. *Leading minds: An anatomy of leadership*. New York: Basic Books.

George, B. 2003. *Authentic leadership: Rediscovering the secrets to creating lasting value*. San Francisco: WileyPublishing House.

George, W. 2007. *True north: Discover your authentic leadership*. San Francisco: Jossey-Bass.

Guber, P. 2007. The four truths of the storyteller. *Harvard Business Review*, December issue.

Inam, H. 2015. *Wired for authenticity: Seven practices to inspire, adapt and lead.* iUniverse.

Josselson, R. 1993. A narrative introduction. In *The narrative study of lives*, ed. R. Josselson and A. Lieblich, vol. 1. Cambridge: Sage.

Keller, J. 2003. Parental Images as a guide to leadership sense making: An attachment perspective on implicit leadership theories. *The Leadership Quarterly* 14: 141–160.

Kiel, F. 2015. *Return on character: The real reason leaders and their companies win.* MA: Harvard Business Review Press.

Kotter, J.P., and H. Rathgeber. 2006. *Our iceberg is melting: Changing and succeeding under any conditions.* New York: St. Martin's Press.

Ligon, G.S., S. Hunter, and M.D. Mumford. 2008. Development of outstanding leadership: A life narrative approach. *The Leadership Quarterly* 19: 312–334.

McAdams, D.P. and McLean, K.C. 2013. Narrative Identity. *Current Directions in Psychological Science* 22 (3):233–238.

Mumford, M.D., and G.G. Manley. 2003. Putting the development in leadership development: Implications for theory and practice. In *The future of leadership development*, ed. S. Murphy, and R.R. Riggio, 237–262. Mahwah, NJ: Erlbaum.

McAdams, D.P. 2014. Leaders and their life stories. In *Conceptions of leadership: Enduring ideas and emerging insights*, ed. A. Scott and D.M. Messick. Basingstoke: Palgrave Macmillan.

McAdams, D.P. 2001. The psychology of life stories. *Review of General Psychology* 5: 100–123.

Morgan, G. 1997. *Images of organisation*, 2nd ed. Thousand Oaks, CA: Sage.

Neumeier, M. 2008. *Brand Flip: Why customers now run companies and how to profit from it (voices that matter).* San Francisco: New Riders.

Pillemer, D.B. 1998. *Momentous events, vivid memories.* Cambridge, MA: Harvard University Press.

Pillemer, D.B. 2003. Directive functions of autobiographical memory: The guiding power of the specific episode. *Memory* 11: 193–202.

Reiser, B.J., J.B. Black, and R.P. Abelson. 1985. Knowledge structures in the organization and retrieval of autobiographical memory. *Cognitive Psychology* 17: 89–137.

Reissner, S., V. Pagan, and C. Smith. 2011. 'Our iceberg is melting': Story, metaphor and the management of organisational change. *Culture and Organization* 17 (5): 417–433.

Schwertly, S. 2015. The secret to activating your audiences brain. *Slideshare Blog*. Available online: http://blogslideshare.net.

Shamir, B., D. Dayan-Horesh, and D. Adler. 2005. Leading by biography: Towards a life story approach to the study of leadership. *Leadership* 1 (1): 13–29.

Shamir, B., and G. Eilam. 2005. "What's your story?" A life-stories approach to authentic leadership development. *The Leadership Quarterly* 16 (3): 395–417.

Simmons, A. 2002. *The story factor: Inspiration, influence, and persuasion through the art of storytelling*. New York: Perseus Books.

6

Learning to Lead: A New Model

Abstract The characteristics of leaders and small firms means making time for new learning can be problematic. Yet, it is the ability of these leaders to learn and apply that learning to the business that is the X factor for success or failure. Interweaving theoretical discussions on leadership development in small firms with new empirical research, this chapter presents the Lead2Grow model for the leaders of micro firms. The distinctiveness of the model encompasses the two key critical areas of practice (taking into account the distinctiveness of entrepreneurial leadership and learning for small firms) and the approach to learning (interacting with real people, to resolve and take action on real problems in real time through questioning and reflection).

Keywords Learning to Lead · Lead2Grow model · Micro firms
Leadership development · Small business · Action learning · Business impact · Business support

6.1 Introduction

There has been limited attention given to issues of leadership development in small firms. Though some argue wider leadership theories can be applied to understand entrepreneurial leadership in this context (e.g. Vecchio 2003), it is logical to assume a need for distinct conceptualisation away from the larger corporate context (Leitch et al. 2009). Building on the foundation of Chaps. 2 and 3, there is no doubt as to the direct correlation of leadership in small firms with business performance and growth, defined as the X factor of success and failure (CMI (Chartered Management Institute) 2015). For micro firms (with less than 10 employees or no employees), taking into account the resource-based theory of organisational competitiveness, it can be argued that their underlying unique competitive advantage is most certainly centred on their capacity to learn (Barney et al. 2001; Ruiz-Mercader et al. 2006; Kelliher and Reinl 2009) and their ability to transfer this learning to the organisation (Jones et al. 2014). Understanding the inadequacy of existing leadership development programmes in meeting the needs of small business owners, as well as limited attention in the literature (with the exception of research by Leitch et al. 2009, 2013; Barnes et al. 2015), this chapter will present a new model of leadership development focused on micro firms.

6.2 Leadership Development in Small Firms

In contrast to a focus on the behaviours and traits of small firm leaders, it is their ability to learn and apply that learning to the organisation that influences business growth (Macpherson and Holt 2007). But, learning for the leaders of small firms is a complex social phenomenon and context-dependent activity arising from participation with others in planned and unplanned activities within and outside the workplace (UKCES (UK Commission for Employment and Skills) 2015). Characterised by a lack of flexibility, engagement, openness and responsiveness, the owners of small firms can encounter difficulties with the requirements of traditional leadership development programmes, which involve time for reflection and feedback (Leitch et al. 2009). This is further complicated by resource limitations for small firms in terms of time and finance, which often means immediate operational needs and activities are often viewed as more important to the leader than making time for new learning.

Looking closer at learning in a micro firm context, it is evident from research by Kelliher and Reinl (2009, 2014) that resource reality only explains in part the emphasis placed on immediately applicable learning. Although this work is not focused on leadership development per se, it does point to a crisis driven approach to learning in micro firms whereby learning occurs as much by accident as by design (Kelliher and Reinl 2014). It is the micro firm's learning culture that lends itself more to informal narrative modes of communication between owner and employees (Penn et al. 1998; Matley 1999). In this way, individual and collective learning competencies are built on the "telling of stories of successful implementation and integration of learning in the workplace" (Reinl and Kelliher 2010, p. 146–147). Further challenges are also evident with regard to the leader's ability to be truly reflexive. Considering the multifaceted demands faced by micro firms means the skill of reflection is often undervalued (Perren 1999; Simpson 2001; Kelliher and Reinl 2009).

In view of these issues, there is substantial evidence pointing to the importance of on-the-job, experiential learning for small business owner managers arising from participation in working activities and interaction with suppliers, customers, employees and others (e.g. Gibb 1997; Perren and Grant 2001; Anderson et al. 2004; Kempster and Cope 2010). For small firms much of the unplanned, incidental learning arises out of dealing with specific contingencies that threaten business performance on an ad hoc basis (Patton and Marlow 2002). More so, there are very good reasons why small business owners prefer to learn in this way. Learning directly related to routine and everyday practice makes it immediately relevant to solving real management problems. Principally, it is the relevance and quality of the skills being learned, which help facilitate improved management and working practices (Kitching 2007). Therefore, especially, for micro firms, learning initiatives should focus on analytical and intuitive skill development on the part of the owner, and the development of employees through individualised learning programmes (Kelliher and Reinl 2009).

Notwithstanding the importance of experiential learning by small firm leaders, there is a disconnect with the learning provided in traditional business support development programmes.

As Jones et al. (2014) also point out, there is a need for entrepreneurial leaders to engage in "action" in order to "learn". So, by drawing on the work of key authors who have published lessons learned from the delivery of small firm leadership development programmes (e.g. Leitch et al. 2009; Jones et al. 2014; Barnes et al. 2015), the following discussion will provide insight into the significance of action learning.

6.2.1 Action Learning for Small Firm Leaders

Notwithstanding the lack of agreed definition in the literature, action learning is recognised both as a learning method (with defined processes) and learning ethos (set of abstract principles not attached to any specific type of delivery) (Leitch et al. 2009). By no means a new concept to management education, it is more widespread and accepted by practitioners delivering business support programmes in general, than in academia. But, the attention paid to action learning in the context of entrepreneurial learning and small firms is growing, and the benefits and limitations are much debated in the literature. While there may be a lack of clarity around the definition of action learning, it is known as a context-specific teaching and learning method that develops and takes new forms in response to different situations and scenarios (Leitch et al. 2009). As explained by Barnes et al. (2015) action learning is a social form of learning whereby participants come together to work on issues and share learning, as well as allowing time for critical reflection. Research has demonstrated that despite some weaknesses, if action learning is implemented correctly it can address problems of engagement context and value (Clarke et al. 2006).

The underlying assumption of action learning can be related to transformational learning, reflected in the famous Chinese proverb *"tell me and I forget, show me and I might remember, but directly involve me and I'll make it my own"*. Allowing the curriculum to emerge from the entrepreneur's own issues and context enables participants in leadership development programmes to explore practical solutions on a daily basis (Jones et al. 2014). The emphasis on peer learning is fundamental to the ethos of action learning, which marks the shift away from a class-room based, one-directional, transmission model of teaching and learning where the teacher chooses the material to be delivered (Leitch et al. 2009). The action-learning group is defined as a community of practice, knowledge is co-constructed between delegates and facilitators (Barnes et al. 2015) by supporting the process of sharing information and experiences to find answers and solve problems (Lave and Wenger 1991; Barnes et al. 2015). In this community of practice individuals can learn from authentic experts with credibility i.e. other entrepreneurs or small business owners in a supportive yet challenging environment (Jones et al. 2014).

The acquisition of new knowledge and skills by the small business leader on a development programme while important will not result in transformation or long term benefits for the firm unless there is collective learning through critical reflexivity (Jones et al. 2010). While action learning can support the critical reflexive process of learning for small business leaders, there is no guarantee that organisational learning will follow. Referred by some as the 'transfer problem' (Saks and Belcourt 2006), for small business leaders it is critical that learning transfer continues after the end of the programme, affecting employees and other stakeholders individually and collectively in the review and revising of work practices (Jones et al. 2014). Research points to the importance of 'strategic space' for learning transfer with real impact as enabled by the development of relationships inside and outside the firm, embedding learning within new routines and systems, the delegation of responsibilities, and adoption of appropriate technologies (Jones et al. 2010).

6.3 Exploring a Solution for Micro Firms

Following experience of working with micro businesses in a major region of the UK, the following discussion will tell the author's story of the design, delivery and evaluation of a bespoke leadership development programme for two cohorts of potential high growth micro firm leaders.

6.3.1 Gap Analysis

It was evident in 2015 that the current provision of leadership development training provided by business support organisations (whether government funded or otherwise) addressed general management and team leadership issues, more relevant to medium sized firms with a management structure than very small or micro firms. It is well known that leaders of micro firms encounter specific and unique challenges in learning that require a bespoke learning approach.

These issues underpinned by constrained financial resources, render the current offer of generic leadership development programmes unsuitable for micro firm leaders. Yet, policy clearly points out the need for the owners of these firms (the vital 95% according to Lord Young in 2013) to engage in leadership and management training necessary to improve performance and grow the business. This in turn should yield a wider and positive economic impact (as per the arguments set out in Chaps. 2 and 3). Given that for micro firms, business performance is a function of managerial competence (Kelliher and Reinl 2009), the focus of the new programme was on the development and learning potential of the leader as key criteria of increased productivity. Moreover, since leadership capability for micro firms is associated with entrepreneurial skills (BIS (Department of Business, Innovation and Skills) Report 2015), the programme also involved the development of entrepreneurial leadership capabilities linked to improving sustainable business performance.

It was the significance of the problem and the relevance of the proposed solution that successfully attracted funding from the UKCES in 2015. The partnership between Causeway Enterprise Agency and Ulster University Business School co-created the first Lead2Grow programme for micro firms in Northern Ireland, which involved two programme cohorts. Traditionally, for University institutions, there is an additional barrier to engagement with micro business entrepreneurs who most often perceive support as too academic and distant from real business practice. However, this partnership proved to be both an attractive and relevant solution for micro firm owners.

6.3.2 Designing the Solution

Programme design is found a critical variable influencing learning by leaders and the transfer of the learning in the business (Jones et al. 2014).

In the context of small firms, as underlined by Barnes et al. (2015) there is a need to understand leadership intent (what the owner thinks leadership is) for practical impact (how the owner practices leadership in their business).

Lead2Grow sought to simplify the strategy of business growth of small firms by focusing on identifying leadership purpose that spans personal and professional spheres of life (Craig and Snooks 2014). The programme was designed on the premise that determination to be self-educated is one of the greatest tactics to get through turbulent times. Key objectives of the programme were to both improve micro firm leadership skills (i.e. self-awareness encompassing motivation, cognition, values and emotional intelligence) and entrepreneurship skills (i.e. action through customer orientation and market opportunities). Secondly, to identify key success measures of improved entrepreneurial leadership capability that stimulates sustained improved business performance for micro firms. Thirdly, to share learning and project results with other micro firm employers and relevant stakeholders across the region for greater economic impact.

As Caniels and Romijn (2003) suggest, business support that connect firms to industry level knowledge should not be a blanket initiative but a targeted activity aimed at progressive, or high growth firms. Therefore, in the recruitment of participants for the Lead2Grow programme, a three stage selection process was adopted: the firms must be micro sized with less than 10 employees, operating in an industry sector defined as potential high growth by InvestNI, and the owner entrepreneur committed to growing the business. The programme was promoted at the first leadership conference for small business in Northern Ireland as well as through local business support networks. This involved working with partners (Department of Education and Learning, Causeway Enterprise Agency, Council, and Enterprise Northern Ireland) to ensure a shared learning agenda that delivered 2 cohorts in two distinct phases of the programme over a 6 month period. All leaders committed a small financial investment to register for the programme (15 on phase one of the programme and 21 on phase two).

In recognition of the programme's more unique approach, it was important to manage expectations from the outset to ensure buy-in from micro firm leaders (defined by the UKCES as hard employers).

This was achieved by working closely with the Causeway Enterprise Agency to promote the programme, taking advantage of their reputation for delivering relevant business support to the region and through their network. In addition, engagement also involved a three-prong strategy. First, highlighting the distinction of Lead2Grow from mainstream/typical business support programmes by explaining leadership is inside out job so less focus on developing specific hard skills and qualifications and more about accepting the programme as a space of personal and strategic change, which may involve vulnerability but ultimately real business impact. Secondly, encouraging delegates to trust the process and allow time and space to learn during and outside specific module and most importantly to enjoy the programme. Thirdly, understanding the time pressures and demands of running a micro business means that time away from the business comes at a financial and timely cost- for some means they are the only person working in the business (i.e. sole trader) or for others, they have only a few employees to rely on while they are out of the business.

The rationale for delivering two cohorts as different phases of the programme was to test and refine the learning based on the learning needs of the micro firm leader. Figure 6.1 presents the key features of phase one of the Lead2Grow programme.

Phase one of Lead2Grow was a shorter and more intense two day version of the programme designed to help a cohort of 15 micro firm leaders overcome any concerns about taking time out of the business, with mentoring taking place after the end of the main two day training event.

The short and more targeted approach of phase one over a 6 week period included:

- Baseline diagnostic interview
- 2 consecutive day programme
- 2 hour one session of mentoring
- Option to attend one day sales leadership academy (outside the time frame of the programme)
- Option to attend half day social media workshop (outside the time frame of the programme)
- Final celebration event (showcasing success of delegates and programme evaluation)

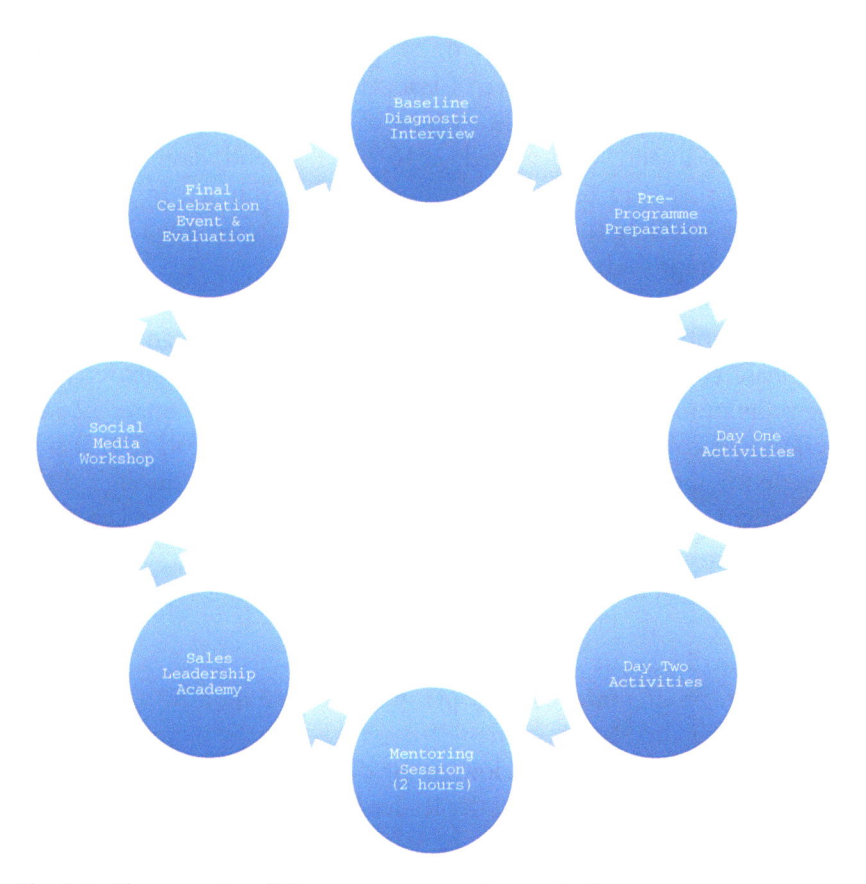

Fig. 6.1 Phase one Lead2Grow programme. *Source* Authors own

The two consectutive day programme included content relating to the story of leadership process presented in Chap. 5. The first day of the programme involved finding the purpose of the leader, which required the development of self-awareness skills through reflection on life stories and feedback from peers in their learning set. The focus on transformational learning events by exploring crucible moments then reframing these events to discover the passion to lead (George 2007) was important in defining leadership purpose. For instance, for some this was a new job, significant reversal in professional or personal life, or a crisis, but whatever the event, it shoed the real plot in the leader's story. This enabled the facilitator to tap into the emotional aspects of learning for micro business leaders (Jones et al. 2014). The first day of activities also involved defining the narrative of leadership purpose encompassing the personal and professional dimensions of their life (Craig and Snooks 2014; Russell and Underwood 2016) The second day was focused on telling the story of leadership purpose underpinned by a practical dimension enabling the micro firm leaders to charge of their purpose in a way that improved performance of the business.

Evaluation data from phase one (comparing base line interviews with final evaluation data) was analysed and identified some changes required for phase two in terms of content and delivery. Overall, phase two of the programme was delivered in more depth and over a longer 12 week period to a cohort of 21 delegates, similar to Barnes et al. (2015) lived experience approach of formal and situational learning through different activities over a protracted time. Figure 6.2 presents the key activities delivered in phase two.

This included the following activities:

- Baseline diagnostic interview
- 3 × day programme (one day per month over 3 months)
- 3 × lunch and learn sessions
- 3 × 2 hour mentoring sessions at the delegate's workplace
- Option to attend one day sales leadership academy (outside the time frame of the programme)
- Option to attend half day social media workshop (outside the time frame of the programme)
- Final celebration event (showcasing success of delegates)

The content for phase two was similar to day one and day two of phase one, but with restructured based on feedback from phase one. Mentoring over a longer period of time proved critical for the business leaders in terms of accountability for actions and embedding of the learning in the organisation. But in phase one of the programme the allocated time was limited to one two hour session, whereas in phase two more time was resourced. In addition, evaluation revealed delegates wanted more time for reflection and action planning in preparation for mentor meetings. Delegates in the second cohort also felt the finance

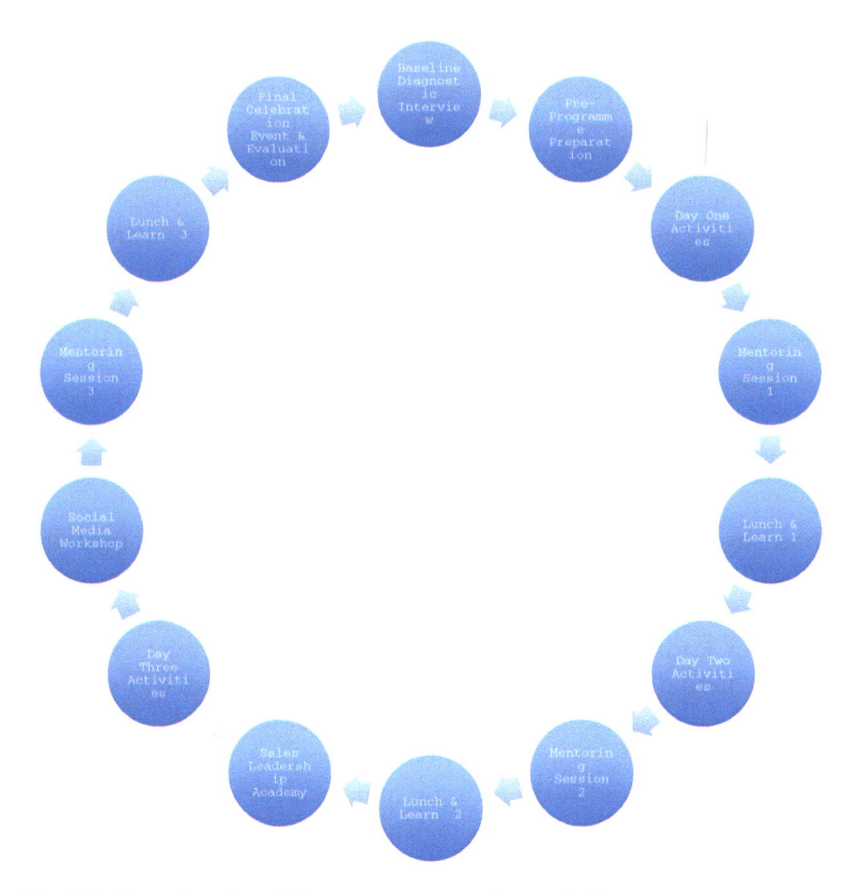

Fig. 6.2 Phase two Lead2Grow programme. *Source* Authors own

session didn't flow with the rest of the content and activities, so this was removed allowing more time for business improvement and customer focused activities. Day three included a new "Learning from leaders" session, which was identified as one of the highlights of the programme providing real inspiration for the subsequent action planning workshop and the extended time spent on developing a relevant and timely plan for the future.

Additional workshops provided opporunities for extended and deeper learning focused on improving the leader's marketing and sales skills, in response to the needs of the delegates on the programme.

Sales was found to be an integral part of the business improvement process and through improved sales techniques, the micro business owner is better placed to grow turnover and profitability, hence delivering on the entrepreneurial skills objective of the programme. Given the prominence of digital media as a marketing tool, the second workshop was also important in the further development of these entrepreneurial skills for leadership in micro businesses. The final celebration event was an important 'story telling' event for delegates, mentors, facilitators and the steering group, as well as other stakeholders, in communicating the lessons learned, the business benefits and impact.

6.3.3 Learning from Harvard

Defined as context-innovation, the Lead2Grow programme used the Harvard Business School purpose driven leadership development ethos (as discussed in Chap. 4) adapted in content and delivery to a programme of learning for the entrepreneurial leaders of micro firms in Northern Ireland. Acknowledging the high profile failures and scandals in the business world, it is very much evident that playing the short-term game of seeking profits only results in ultimate failure of the business. So, for entrepreneurial leaders the focus on improvement should not be confined to making a profit only, but making a bigger and wider difference. For entrepreneurial leaders of micro business organistions, this model of purpose driven leadership offers a different perspective, encompassing an internal focus on the leader's sweet spot (at the intersection of where the leader is highly motivated and his/her core strengths). But, understanding the need for immediate and relevant learning for purposes of business impact, Lead2Grow also developed practical content according to the needs of the leaders on the programme (such as the workshops) to ensure relevance for the purposes of learning transfer for the benefit of the whole organisation, including meeting the needs of customers and suppliers in a long term and sustainable way.

At the outset of the programme, this model was considered theoretically relevant for 2 reasons. According to Harvard research, purpose is touted as the key to navigating the complex volatile and ambiguous world today, where strategy is ever changing and few decisions are obviously right or wrong. Secondly, It has found that while larger corporate firms are able to point to policies designed to underpin their sense of purpose, for smaller firms, purpose is something innate. As explained in Chap. 4, research conducted in the UK highlights examples of micro firms who have achieved high growth in mobilising their purpose (CMI (Chartered Management Institute) 2014). For these firms to find the motivation to lead and the energy to persist in the face of obstacles and setbacks, they must operate from strong convictions and high level of purpose.

6.4 Pedagogic Review

A focus on immediately applicable learning (as evident in the majority of generic leadership and management programmes for SMEs), has been found to be detrimental to the long-term leadership development and performance. The Lead2Grow programme on other hand sought to mirror micro firm culture by leveraging an informal individual and collective learning environment by adopting an action learning approach in the delivery of training and mentoring. In this way it was a personal learning lab for the micro business leader incorporating a multidimensional learning approach and a wide range of learning opportunities and tools including:

- Learning log: private and confidential manual for delegates to write notes, ideas, plan and keep ongoing record of personal development and changes to implement in the business
- Learning sets: peer-to-peer learning through group activities giving and receiving feedback and building trust over time
- Networking: between micro business leaders within learning set and with wider cohort during extended break times
- Individual reflection: taking time out from the haze and noise of busyness and multitasking to find clarity on how to better lead the business
- Storytelling by successful leaders: the lessons learned in growing the business from small beginnings to larger scale was important to provide role models and encouragement to participants

- Support: role of mentors outside module delivery proved an accountability function not only to give expert advice and provide honest feedback, but supporting leaders to keep on track to achieve goals
- Short clinics/master classes: transfer of new knowledge in key areas in short 30 minute sessions

While resource limitations can promote urgent operational needs over new learning for micro firm leaders, the approach of Lead2Grow encouraged interaction between business owners, resolving and taking action on real problems in real time and learning through knowledge transfer, questioning and reflection. Leadership in small firms is a socially constructed process learnt through social interactions, not necessarily in a conscious manner (Kempster 2009), therefore in this way the social dimension of learning sets approach sought to address the loneliness of leadership indicative of micro firms. In the Lead2Grow programme, the approach of bringing together businesses at a similar stage of development (i.e. length of time in business) was effective given that learning needs differed according to life stage of the business. This then formed a community of practice within each programme as well as within learning sets as participants engaged in common activity and formed shared meanings through problem solving.

Mentoring was particularly important for leaders throughout the programme, allowing for the embedding of learning in the workplace through process of development and change in practice and knowledge. Categorised as double loop learning, leaders were encouraged to ask why something works, or not, and from their mentor obtain new insights and patterns about a proposed solution, then trialing this in everyday business. Mentoring was also important in helping the leaders of micro business to reflect on the lessons learned from the mentor in light of their own practice and business needs (Kempster and Cope 2010). In phase two, mentoring occurred in between the main sessions, which allowed delegates to act on and apply the lessons learned, actively working towards achieving key goals (identified as important by Leitch et al. 2009). A critical component of the mentoring was the plan for action and change, important to ensure the leaders developed their critical thinking skills in order to improve leadership capability.

But, the positive benefits of the mentoring depended on the right match (or rapport) between micro business leader and the designated mentor.

6.5 Lead2grow Model

The Lead2Grow model of micro business leadership development was formed from the purpose driven leadership approach discussed in Chap. 4 and data collected throughout the 6 month period of programme delivery. Data was gathered from the learning at each phase of the programme with delegates using interviews, questionnaires, evaluation surveys, focus group, and observation data. Data analysis involved triangulation by the Project Coordinator, Project Champions, Project Manager and Steering Group to ensure the reliability and validity of findings. From the testing of the Lead2Grow pilot in two phases, specific learning in terms of content and delivery to ensure engagement and impact was critical in refining not only the programme offering, but the Lead2Grow model presented in Fig. 6.3.

At the center of the model, the leader's purpose is aligned to internal and external focus of business activities (process improvement and customer management), underpinned by the leader's knowledge/skills (IQ) and emotional intelligence (EQ). For micro business leaders, the strategy of business growth was simplified by focusing on finding, defining and telling leadership purpose spanning both personal and professional spheres of life. The re-integration of the leader's personal and business roles was identified as a key recommendation for further development of action learning in leadership development programmes (Leitch et al. 2009). The premise at the core of leadership development for micro firms stems from understanding that leading any business is first an 'inside job'. The purpose piece of the programme was found to be very powerful for micro business leaders and early resistance was broken down once they started to define their own purpose, in day one of the programme, which improved individual motivation for the rest of the programme.

The objectives of the programme were to improve leadership skills and entrepreneurship skills in order to stimulate sustained improved

Fig. 6.3 Lead2Grow model. *Source* Authors own

business performance for micro firms. Therefore, combining the exploration of leadership purpose with practice in leading the customer and leading business improvement in key areas enabled real impact for the firm (the results will be discussed in the next section). Adopting the principles of marginal gains theory, understanding and identifying the small internal changes that need to happen yielded larger gains in improvement and greater impact over time for the business. There is no business without customers, thus, the external focus on leading sustainable value creation is important in safeguarding purpose not only for profit, but purpose also defined in making a difference for the customer and other stakeholders of the firm. This happens when the customer or stakeholder is connected to the why of the business and its leader. As such, these practical master class sessions prompted leaders to focus efforts in linking their leadership learning to functional and strategic aspects of their business (Jones et al. 2014).

Finally, the personal and professional focus of model is defined by leadership excellence including both IQ (knowledge/expertise) and EQ (emotional intelligence) skills. Essentially, this starts with self-awareness i.e. leading with excellence first themselves before leading others (employees, customers, shareholders). Action learning in the programme is critical to achieving excellence that transcends the personal and professional lives of the leader after the programme. Acknowledging the learning transfer problem for small business leaders, mentoring between main sessions provided feedback on the experimentation of new strategies and made certain that learning and development of the leader's skills continued. This in turn facilitated the transfer of learning to the organisation by working through new plans of action aligned to their leadership purpose with their employees, customers and suppliers to improve performance and impact.

6.5.1 Business and Leader Impact

The data from the Lead2Grow research provides evidence that the Harvard purpose driven leadership model is applicable to entrepreneurial leaders of micro firms resulting in improved leadership skills and business performance. In this way, the model supports the original hypothesis of the programme, in that the purpose driven leadership development ethos originating in the USA for large multinational firms is also applicable in a micro firm context yielding real benefits for developing the leader and improving the business. It was the action learning approach of the Lead2Grow programme that allowed micro firm leaders to tailor the content of the curriculum to their own issues and explore practical solutions within their learning set or community of practice. Learning sets were carefully constructed by the facilitator in a way that enabled trust to build between delegates and entrepreneurial leaders did not encounter issues of competition, but rather the background, experience and industry sectors enabled synergy in a supportive yet challenging environment. This also involved evaluation and follow up by the Project Officer and the comparison of learning before and after the programme, which was important in ascertaining real and measurable impact.

From a more practical perspective, in review of the research carried out in both phases of the programme, it was also found that user acceptance and engagement with a new leadership agenda and programme of learning is dependent upon the reputation of the Anchor Institution (in this case Causeway Enterprise Agency) and the language used in promoting the conference and programme. It was also interesting to find that the leaders of micro firms were willing to pay a fee and commit the time to attending both the short and longer version of the leadership programme. Indeed, it was the extended version of the programme with monthly engagement, regular mentoring and varied learning activities and workshops yields greater impact in terms of hard and soft skills for the leader and the improved performance for the business. As such, benefits for the majority of delegates included improved confidence in leading the business and improved ambition to grow the business.

6.5.2 Regional Economic Impact

Lead2Grow is linked to local economic growth in the region in terms of improving the productivity of 36 micro businesses by focusing on the development of their leaders. The focus was for micro businesses to be better at what they do and have an ambition to grow their market (either by improving sales/income or improving effectiveness of processes), not necessarily to grow employees. The KPIs set for this project provide evidence of the practical business focused impact of the programme in addition to the softer skills dimension of leader confidence and ambition. It is this dual approach that ensures impact at business level, which in accumulation with the rest of the 36 micro firms over time, will in turn impact the future regional economy.

In terms of extended impact in the region, the two workshops were opened to small business owners outside Lead2Grow delegates. For the Sales Leadership workshop there was 96 in attendance across both days and 72 were non-Lead2Grow participants. The social media workshop had 46 in attendance and 13 were non-Lead2Grow participants (and not the same employers who attended sales leadership academy).

Therefore, given the significant attendance of business leaders beyond Lead2Grow at both workshops the wider improvement in leadership skills will yield a growth in existing and new market opportunities for all local businesses that attended.

6.6 Summary Chapter

Building on previous chapters, discussion herein has focused on exploring an emergent solution for leadership development in the micro firm context. Understanding that competitive advantage is centered on the micro business leader's capacity to learn and then transfer that learning across the business for real impact, there is acknowledgment of the disconnect with traditional methods of learning in mainstream business support programmes. Existing knowledge generated by research in the field of leadership development and small business has pointed to the relevance of action research in overcoming problems of engagement, context and value (e.g. Clarke et al. 2006; Leitch et al. 2009; Jones et al. 2014; Barnes et al. 2015). But, these studies have focused on small firms with more than 20 employees and/or high performing firms. Focusing on the micro firm, underrepresented in terms of existing knowledge of leadership development in the literature, this chapter has presented and explained the significance of the Lead2Grow model for improved performance and impact.

References

Anderson, N., C.K.W. de Drew, and B.A. Nijstad. 2004. The Routinization of Innovation Research: A Constructively Critical Review of the State-of-the-Science. *Journal of Organizational Behavior* 25: 147–173.

Barnes, S., S. Kempster, and S. Smith. 2015. *LEADing Small Business: Business Growth through Leadership Development*. London: Edward Elgar Publishing Ltd.

Barney, J., M. Wright, and D.J. Ketchen. 2001. The Resource-Based View of the Firm: Ten Years after 1991. *Journal of Management* 27: 625–641.

BIS (Department of Business, Innovation and Skills) Report. 2015. *Leadership and Management Skills in Small and Medium-Sized Businesses* Ref: BIS/15/95.

Caniels, M., and H.A. Romijn. 2003. SME Clusters, Acquisition of Technological Capabilities and Development: Concepts, Practice and Policy Lesson. *Journal of Industry Competition and Trade* 3 (3): 187–210.

Clarke, J., R. Thorpe, L. Anderson, and J. Gold. 2006. It's all Action, it's all Learning: Action Learning in SMEs. *Journal of European Industrial Training* 30 (6): 441–455.

CMI (Chartered Management Institute). 2014. Management 2020 Report: Leadership to Unlock Long-term Growth. *The Commission on the Future of Leadership and Management.*

CMI (Chartered Management Institute). 2015. Growing Your Small Business: The Role of Business Schools and Professional Bodies. *Chartered Management Institute Publication*, September.

Craig, N., and S. Snooks. 2014. From Purpose to Impact: Figure Out Your Passion and Put It to Work. *Harvard Business Review* 92 (5): 105–111.

Gibb, A.A. 1997. Small Firms' Training and Competitiveness. Building upon the Small Business as a Learning Organisation. *International Small Business Journal* 14 (3): 13–29.

George, W. 2007. *True north: discover your authentic leadership*. San Francisco: Jossey-Bass.

Jones, O., A. Macpherson, and R. Thorpe. 2010. Learning in Owner-managed Small Firms: Mediating Artefacts and Strategic Space. *Entrepreneurship and Regional Development* 22 (7): 649–673.

Jones, K., S. Sambrook, H.A. Pittaway, and H. Norbury. 2014. Action Learning: How Learning Transfers from Entrepreneurs to Small Firms. *Action Learning: Research and Practice* 11 (2): 131–166.

Kelliher, F., and L. Reinl. 2009. A Resource-Based View of Micro-Firm Management Practice. *Journal of Small Business and Enterprise Development* 16 (3): 521–532.

Kelliher, F., and L. Reinl. 2014. The Social Dynamics of Micro-Firm Learning in an Evolving Learning Community. *Tourism Management* 40: 117–125.

Kempster 2009. Observing the Invisible: Examining the Role of Observational Learning in the Development of Leadership Practice. *Journal of Management Development* 28 (5): 439–456.

Kempster, S., and J. Cope. 2010. Learning to Lead in the Entrepreneurial Context. *International Journal of Entrepreneurial Behaviour and Research* 16 (1): 5–34.

Kitching, J. 2007. Regulating Employment Relations Through Workplace Learning: A Study of Small Employers. *Human Resource Management Journal* 17 (1): 42–57.

Lave, J., and E. Wenger. 1991. *Situated Learning: Legitimate Peripheral Participation*. Cambridge: Cambridge University Press.

Leitch, C., C. McMullan, and R.T. Harrison. 2009. Leadership Development in SMEs: An Action Learning Approach. *Action Learning: Research and Practice* 6 (3): 243–263.

Leitch, C.M., C. McMullan, and R.T. Harrison. 2013. The Development of Entrepreneurial Leadership: The Role of Human, Social and Institutional Capital. *British Journal of Management* 24: 347–366.

Macpherson, A., and R. Holt. 2007. Knowledge, Learning and Small Firm Growth: A Systematic Review of the Evidence. *Research Policy* 36: 172–192.

Matlay, H. 1999. Employee Relations in Small Firms: A Micro-Business Perspective. *Employee Relations* 21 (3): 285.

Patton, D., and S. Marlow. 2002. The Determinants of Management Training Within Smaller Firms in the UK. What Role Does Strategy Play? *Journal of Small Business and Enterprise Development* 9 (3): 260–270.

Penn, D.W., W. Angiwa, R. Forster, G. Heydon, and S.J. Richardson. 1998. Learning in Small Organisations. *The Learning Organization* 5 (3): 128–137.

Perren, L. 1999. Factors in the Growth of Micro-Enterprises, Part 1: Developing a Framework. *Journal of Small Business and Enterprise Development* 6 (4): 366–385.

Perren, L., and P. Grant. 2001. *Management and Leadership in UK SMEs: Witness Testimonies From the World of Entrepreneurs and SME Managers*. London: Council for Excellence in Management and Leadership.

Reinl, L., and F. Kelliher. 2010. Cooperative Micro-Firm Strategies: Leveraging Resources Through Learning Networks. *International Journal of Entrepreneurship and Innovation* 11 (2): 141–150.

Ruiz-Mercader, J., A.L. Meron~o-Cerdan, and R. Sabater-Sanchez. 2006. Information Technology and Learning: Their Relationship and Impact on Organisational Performance in Small Businesses. *International Journal of Information Management* 26: 16–29.

Russell, E. and Underwood, C. 2016. Exploring the role of purpose. *HR Magazine*, 1 June.

Saks, A.M., and M. Belcourt. 2006. An Investigation of Training Activities and Transfer of Training in Organisations. *Human Resource Management* 45: 629–648.

Simpson, B. 2001. Innovation and the Micro-Enterprise. *International Journal of Services Technology and Management* 2 (3–4): 377–387.

UKCES (UK Commission for Employment and Skills). 2015. *Developing Leadership and Entrepreneurship skills in small firms: How can anchor Institutions Support the Development of Small Firms in their Local Economy?* March.

Vecchio, R.P. 2003. Entrepreneurship and Leadership: Common Trends and Common Threads. *Human Resource Management Review* 13: 303–327.

7

Storytelling: Starting Out

Abstract Understanding the high failure rate of small businesses in the first five years, this chapter tells the story of entrepreneurial small business leadership early in their formation. Unlike the approach of traditional case studies told with the benefit of hindsight, the insight by four entrepreneurial leaders in this chapter provides a captivating account of leadership development in starting out. Regardless of industry sector, the stories reveal a golden thread personified in the leader's self-awareness, resilience and ambition in that they know their purpose and are growing their business against the odds.

Keywords Storytelling · Entrepreneurial leaders · Leadership development · Purpose · Learning to lead · Metaphorical expression Surfing · Luxury handbags · Childcare · Technology solutions

© The Author(s) 2018
K. Hutchinson, *Leadership and Small Business*,
DOI 10.1007/978-3-319-64777-7_7

7.1 Introduction

The book to this point has provided discussion of small business leadership from the perspectives of the organisation, the entrepreneur, through leadership theory, as well as an introduction to the relevance of storytelling. The current chapter tells the story of leading small business by the entrepreneurs who make sense of their leadership development in a small business still 'under construction'. In this specific region of the UK, Northern Ireland has lower than average rates of both creation and survival of start-ups. Four remarkable entrepreneurial leaders tell their story in the moment of leading their business. While different types of owners have different traits, behaviour, and motivations for the businesses, these business owners all have a substantive ambition to grow, which is met with the determination, opportunity and effective leadership skills to make it happen. Metaphorical expression is used to bring the narratives of these entrepreneurial leaders to life.

7.2 Karen Yates: Taylor Yates

Taylor Yates is a social good business designing and selling luxury handbags with a special story. Already the owner of another business, Karen Yates, the founder of Taylor Yates discovered her innate desire to find a meaningful purpose in business when preparing for a guest lecture at her local University. It all started with the realisation that she was looking for something that was missing in the market followed by a conversation with her daughter, which uncovered the need for beautiful bags with a beautiful purpose. Now in the second year of business, after considerable time at the design stage she has recently launched her new product line into the market. She speaks still at the starting line about the vulnerability in leading a new venture and bravery required to start the race without knowing what the next lap of the competition will bring for her and her company.

Image 7.1 Karen Yates

7.2.1 Finding a Purpose

My husband and I have owned a small print and design family business for over 15 years inherited from my father-in-law who started it in 1960. But, it was in 2015 when I really discovered a new purpose wrapped in a new business venture. I was asked to give a lecture at a local university about ethics in marketing, but this invitation proved much more than an opportunity for the undergraduate students to learn from a female business leader. It was a sea change in my working life leading me in a completely new and meaningful direction. As I began my research in preparation for the lecture I became more and more aware that the world of business had changed, and leadership as a concept and behaviour was also changing. I was truly inspired. I could see how the growing irrelevance of twentieth century systems and the big shift in values was bringing community back to the heart of business. I connected to this new wave of thinking and doing business. It reminded me of where I grew up in the north of England a place where family, honesty, and hard work were the backbone of community.

This revelation coincided with planning for my daughter's 18th birthday. I wanted to mark her birthday with a special gift and I thought maybe a designer handbag. To me a handbag is a personal purchase, a symbol of love and belonging to be cherished for many years. I had to be a beautiful product, but understated. So, I searched and searched, but I could see nothing I liked or I knew she would like and appreciate. I found the marketplace saturated and dominated by large corporates and while some give back in a small way, I could see the need a product and business were giving back was the intention from the beginning. For many girls, the first designer handbag is a right of passage, and for my daughter I wanted to be part of that right of passage. But, more so I wanted it to be about the freedom of choice. I wanted the girl who could afford the handbag to give the girl who can't the freedom of choice. Knowing the world was crying out for products and services rooted in a bigger purpose of kindness and community collided with the need to find a beautiful and understated gift for my daughter and that's how my purpose was born.

I have always worked for larger companies in a range of sectors from clothing manufacturing to multinational retailers. Even though we owned our own business, because we took over the family firm it always felt like I was working for someone else. Now in discovering the idea for a new business intertwined with a purpose beyond profit, led to a greater re-discovery of my roots. I had forgotten women determined to make life better surrounded me in my childhood who looked after each other and others in our community. I had denied my roots for a very long time believing I needed to in order to disassociate with the struggle of a working class background. So in mobilising my purpose in Taylor Yates, it has meant going back in order to spring forward. The name of my business is fittingly named after those great women in my family. More so, I have realised my life had more purpose than I thought it had, it was more set out for me than I had every imagined and it feels like I have come full circle, now deeply connected back to my roots.

7.2.2 Role Models and Game Changers

It takes determination, resilience and a lot of hard work to be in any business today and in the last two years I have been reminded of the strong Lancashire women that guided me and gave me the freedom to choose. I realised my Nana, Alice Wells, among others had showed me another way. She started in service in Yorkshire in the 1920's but went on to run three businesses from her home. We spent every summer there as children and sometimes I accompanied her on buying trips to the wholesalers. She was tenacious as well as being fiercely independent and I have been told I inherited some of her hard working northern grit. Other great women in my life included my mum who was glamorous, fiercely loyal, kind and worked hard like her mother, Alice. I also remember Doris who lived next door and ran the local hairdressers at the end of Alice's garden. She was known as the salt of the earth friend and neighbour who spent Saturday mornings chatting and styling the hair of local women in the surrounding area. Bottom line: they may not have led a life of luxury, but they were happy and content playing their part in the local community. I mention only a few of the strong women I remember, but I know they all played an important part in role modeling leadership in business to me.

7.2.3 Recessionary Learning

I have spent much of my career in business running around and doing. Focus, reflection and structure do not come easily, but I have learned these are vital in leading and growing any business. I went to University and have engaged in formal learning, but it wasn't until my husband and I experienced our biggest crisis in the family business during the recession, that we learned the biggest lesson as leaders. One day not long after it the recession was announced, we sat in front of the bank manager who told us we were leaking cash and it was only a matter of weeks before the business would go under. We had 17 employees at the time and we had only a few days to come up with a plan or the business would go under and quicker than we knew. It was shock. We didn't know how good life was up until that point. We didn't really have a firm grip on all of the financial details of our business in the way we should. I learned that the numbers and details around the business are crucial and it is the ability to bounce back from the shock and find a plan B or C or D that is the right solution is all that really matters.

Change is always constant in business. So, learning how to come back after a shock with the right strategic move has been critical in growing Taylor Yates. We launched at Christmas with pre-ordered stock and I understood we could call off stock in small numbers. But, then it all changed and suddenly I was told to buy in bulk. It meant I was faced with finding a serious amount of cash in a very short period of time. I knew I had to be confident in my ability as a leader to make the right decision and I wouldn't have known how to do that if I hadn't been through it before. The confidence and bravery required to lead a new fledgling business has grown since I became part of a CEO membership group called Vistage. Monthly meetings with world class speakers who bring new knowledge and the peer learning in my group has given me energy to keep motivated as well as a hunger to learn more. The accountability function of this group makes sure that I bring the learning back into business both for short-term solutions and longer term impact.

7.2.4 Leading at the Starting Line

As a teenager I ran for the county, in many heats and in many competitions across the UK. Each time before I ran a race I had to auto assess my position in the field against competitors and muster the bravery and energy to step up to the starting line. For me, establishing Taylor Yates has felt like a new race, a new competition surrounded by lots of supporters in the audience. Starting a new business that is truly mine is like getting into those starting blocks again and at this early stage of the firm, it is necessary that I find the self belief to lead from the front and win the race again. The determination and sheer stubbornness to get to the starting line I know I inherited from the strong women I grew up with who showed me it can be done. The women that we grew up with gave us the freedom to choose our own path, we would like to try and do the same. That is why every product we sell will give back something that we believe will have a positive impact in the world. So knowing there is a business rooted in a bigger purpose gives me the strength to endure the grueling training in preparation for the next step of growth.

Knowing that I am not alone but can train with other business owners, is an important part of the training regime and one that can make the difference between a gold, silver and bronze medal.

I spent two years designing and creating the perfect beautiful product confident it was ready for the market. Yet, when it came to the launch date of the new product line only 5 months ago, I was overwhelmed with the fear no one would like it in the way I liked it. I had to deliver something of worth that felt good for us as a business and for our customers. But, accepting vulnerability was part of the package of leading a new business in a new market; I had no choice but to just go for it and ended up selling 30% of my stock in 30 days! While at the outset the business plan identified online selling as the primary place of doing business, I realised I also wanted to see the product in shops. So, I have changed the strategy of the business to a bricks and clicks model. But, aligning my product to the right retailer with the same values is everything and not an easy task. I need to secure a partnership with larger retailers on a global scale in order to achieve the economies of scale and protect the margin. So I have identified key high-end retailers where I would like to stock my product and I am presently trying to secure this business. It is a waiting game, but I am determined not to give into stocking products just anywhere staying true to seeing the beautiful purpose of my business grow in a profitable and meaningful way.

For more information on the company visit www.tayloryates.com.

7.3 Ricky Martin: Skunkworks Surf Co

Skunkworks Surf Co. is a small family firm founded by brothers Chris and Ricky Martin, in 2014. The name of the business 'Skunkworks' means a small and loosely structured group of individuals, unhampered by bureaucracy who research and develop a new project for the purpose of radical innovation. For Chris and Ricky it means making the most robust surfboards in the world with minimum negative impact on the environment. Inspired by a deep connection to the sea and frustrated by the short life span of learner surfboards, the brothers worked with some of the UK and Ireland's best engineers, materials and experts to create a strong,

Image 7.2 Ricky and Chris Martin

100% recyclable surfboard, using no glues, adhesives, or resins. With an initial investment of £50,000 SkunkWorks Surf Co. was born. Three years into the business venture Ricky tells the story of leading his award winning company with his brother and how they are growing the family unit to meet the growing demands for their product across the world.

7.3.1 'Blood Brother' Leadership

Chris and I grew up on the Causeway Coast and loved surfing. So much for me that I went on to compete as a body border on the Irish Surf team, as well as in European competitions. Whilst this was my passion, my history of employment included working in a recruitment business for several years, as well as setting up the first surf school on the North Coast. Chris is also a surfer but more of a serial entrepreneur and innovative thinker. I had a major problem with the surfboards in my surf school, and Chris came up with a solution. At that moment, we became more than blood brothers and began a new family adventure.

We are complete opposites in every way, so many people warned us that going into business together would be difficult! At the beginning it was fine, but we reached a crisis point in our relationship one year into the business; it could have caused our business to collapse, but ended up the best thing that ever happened. From that point of self-awareness we each developed a new and deep respect for each other and our relationship has since matured.

From that crisis, we learned two critical lessons: the importance of clearly defined leadership roles and the art of communication. We understand that while we are two very different halves of the whole leadership team, we combine the role well. The great thing is that we are good at different things. I am head of sales and marketing, and Chris leads on product design and production. We both really enjoy what we do and each of us has a lot going on at any one time. This clear distinction between roles is essential and the fact we are both good in our own areas allows us to respect each other's 'patch' of the business, and the business overall benefits from this synergy. Like every marriage, divorce is always a threat if we don't work at it, but the sense of responsibility for our staff makes us stay together and work out our differences for the benefit of growing the business. That said, most of the time we get on great and work really well together—only a few times have we wanted to strap the other to one of our boards and send him out to sea!

7.3.2 Leading from Idea to Reality

We believe products just aren't designed or made to last anymore, and that is really what got us going three years ago. I had owned my own surf school and I was fed up with all of my foam surfboards falling apart after only a few months of being used. It was costing me a fortune. Aware that this problem was a global phenomenon, and armed with a solution thanks to Chris, the mission became all about making the most robust surfboards in the world with minimum negative impact on the environment. The goal was simple, but we had no clue how long or how much work it was going to take to get to where we are now, never mind how much money. Coming up with an idea is one thing, but turning it into a reality is a massive undertaking that—until you try it—you will never be able to comprehend the sheer amount of work involved.

Starting out is never glamorous. In the first year we had two employees that worked for us for free; they took on part-time jobs at weekends to make ends meet. Chris and I had no salary but we couldn't give up even when we wanted to, because we had two other people—friends—committed to us, working for no salary. When we had no energy left, when everything was going wrong, when we were up against it every way we looked, we both thought it was time to give up… but we didn't. Rather, we woke up the next day and kept on fighting for our dream. I think it is the ability to simply keep leading on that makes the difference between failure and success.

Put in the hours and I can tell you it eventually pays off. We didn't rush to market but instead spent two years prototype testing; we have gone through a boat load of design and material changes but we have total and complete confidence in the shape, design, and quality of our boards. With our patent pending heat bonding process, and our painstakingly sourced and tested materials, we have achieved our aim.

We are now in a new 15,000 square foot factory, we have simplified and updated our manufacturing process meaning we can make up to 12 times as many boards in a week as we currently do. This in turn brings our price of production down so we can make all our boards for the world right here at home on the Causeway Coast of Ireland. Located on the bank of the river, not only can we actually arrive to work on a paddleboard, but it means paddle board testing happens 30s after the boards come of the production line!

Staying local is important to us. We have insisted from day one that we would manufacture everything ourselves in Northern Ireland. There are a couple of reasons for this; firstly, we wanted to ensure absolute control over everything from the purchasing of materials to the final product leaving the factory. How can you have quality control when your product is being manufactured on the other side of the world? Secondly, we want to show that it is still possible to manufacture in the UK and Ireland. Our dream was to start something special, create local jobs, and support the local economy. There were so many people in our ear suggesting moving everything to China as we would more profitable. But, no chance—we are staying true to our goal and our community.

7.3.3 Growing the Family

Growing the business for us is like raising a family. Managing the family finances has been critical. Up until recently, our machinery was limiting our business growth, but we couldn't buy the machinery we needed without significant capital. The two year period of research and development was long and expensive for the company, but the critical injection of £500,000 into the business has made all the difference in growing the family unit. We also needed a new and much larger home to accommodate the new machinery to meet the demand for our product. So, last year we moved into a new 15,000 square feet factory. The new machinery brought with it the need for more staff, and within six months, our team trebled in size from four to twelve employees.

Managing relationships within the family business has also proved critical, especially with the significant growth in such a short space of time. Culture is everything to Chris and I, and as we grow our business protecting the culture is a challenge. We have done it, but it isn't always easy. Managing relationships, as in any family, can be challenging, but we have taken a very careful and intentional approach to recruitment in order to find and keep the right people. For our business, it is all about transferrable skills. So for example, we recruited a chef last year to join the production team. Some may wonder what on earth has food got in common with making surfboards? I would say everything. From preparing the food/materials, to setting up each station to assemble the product/make the food, the same skills are required. If I replace the word 'food' for 'foam' our newest recruit is actually doing almost the same job as when he was a chef. But, more than that, he is just a fantastic person with a positive and enthusiastic personality, with no ego and with values aligned to our family culture. In recruiting we use our existing team to find the right people with these traits and behaviours, as well as a work ethic, and this gives our staff a sense of ownership in finding the right people to join our business.

The biggest challenge for us in growing continues to be money, money, and money. We have been really fortunate when it comes to funding but money is always the biggest issue. We have reached out to various organisations and received significant support from Northern Ireland Science Park, Northern Ireland Polymers Association, Queens

University and regional colleges in our adventure. This led to several proofs of concept and R&D grants enabling us to grow to the next stage. Recently, we have brought on board two new partners with a vast wealth of experience and contacts. We now have the best investors ever, who love the product and the business, and most important they believe in our ability to lead. We are even in touch with the experts who do the testing for NASA in California as a result of our mentors. Like our parents, these experts also look out for our health and well-being, advising us on how to take time out for our own families to maintain some balance in the midst of leading a new business.

7.3.4 Award Winning Leadership

An indication of the commercial potential of the company has been our two high profile awards. In 2015, after 6 months battling through round after round of pitching to top entrepreneurs, we fought hard and finally won the top award for excellence in Engineering at Invent—a regional competition run by the Northern Ireland Science Park. Also in 2015, we took part in the world renowned Virgin Media Business Pitch to Rich competition, where I did a pitch for investment to Richard Branson. While we didn't win the overall top award, we were very proud to come runners-up in the "New Things" category of the competition. The award gave us £10,000 investment to perfect our new model of surfboards. But the nationwide competition in reality gave us much more. It served to launch the name, brand, and profile of the company by giving us serious media coverage across the UK and Ireland, in turn building an incredibly supportive and loyal following. This is typified by the fact that one of our two new investors followed our progress on Pitch to Rich, then got in touch to offer potential investment. So while it took a lot of work and dedication to get to the final and pitch to Richard Branson, it remains one of our most worthwhile 'investments' in promoting the company across the whole country.

Looking to the future, the new design of our surfboard is only the starter course on the menu. We have many other R&D projects going on in the background with plans and timelines for launching several new products over the next few years. Ireland has some of the best waves on the planet—now ranked the number one surf destination for many international surfers. In a similar way, I want to see SkunkWorks Surf Co become a global brand in five years. Not for the primary reason to sell out and get as rich as possible, but we want to show the people of the UK, Europe, and the rest of world that we can manufacture products here in Northern Ireland, and make money doing it. I want to encourage other people to bring manufacturing back and stop getting everything made in the Far East. For us the dream is about building community and bringing prosperity back to where we live.

For more information on the company visit www.skunkworkssurf.co.uk.

7.4 Danielle Tagg: Articlave Day Nursery

It all started in April 2014, when Danielle Tagg set out on new adventure to create her own Nursery providing high quality, professional childcare service to the community. It was always about a love for looking after children, but when faced with a significant challenge in her personal life, she knew the way forward was to own her own daycare nursery business. Coming to a new country and overcoming significant challenges in her family life, Danielle has pursued excellence from the outset leading with whole-hearted commitment to making it the best nursery in the region. Only three years in business, she has already received four regional and national leadership awards, strong accolades of her success in growing the company from small beginnings with just her and one other employee to employing a team of 14 staff today. Most significant was her award for Business Woman of the year in 2016. Her story will tell the tale of starting a new business against the odds and how significant investment in her leadership development has been the bedrock of her success to date. As her company goes from strength to strength, she talks about growing the team before growing the business in order to protect the high quality and professional service that puts children at the heart of everything they do.

Image 7.3 Danielle Tagg

7.4.1 Pioneering a New Adventure

I was 26 years old and all I knew was life in Morocco. I knew there was more to see and more to do and I sought adventure. But, I did not seek adventure for adventures sake; I wanted to make the very best life for my future family and me. So in 2003 I left Morocco and my large family and set out to start a new life in Northern Ireland even though my parents begged me to stay. I arrived with a degree from my home country but decided there was much more I wanted to learn so I embarked on some new training and became an interpreter. Some years later I got married and settled down to have my own family, leaving the world of work to focus on my children. But this dream was cut short. My marriage ended. My youngest was eight months old and I had a toddler, was in a wheel chair and had no job. Finding myself a single mother with two young children, with few friends and ostracised by the only family I had known in this country, I had to find a job to fit with looking my family. I am stubborn and while my parents never wanted me to go, I couldn't tell them about the failure of my marriage and the fact I didn't know what I would do to survive. But, I knew I couldn't go back to my old life in Morocco, I loved my life here, and so did my children, so I had to make it work. I had to focus on finding another way to make a better life for us all. So after a few years of teaching assistance in a local primary school, fuelled by a hunger for a new adventure I pioneered my own business venture to build the life I always wanted.

No one believed me. Some told me I was mad, others laughed. There was a cultural perception because of my ethnicity that I was not educated but rather I was stupid and ignorant of the world of business. But, in spite of the negativity, I took the financial left overs from my divorce and invested all I had in setting up the business. I pressed ahead and alone to take on premises on a site renowned in the local area for a series of business failure. I was determined to turn the tide on the past not just for me personally to achieve the financial independence I always wanted, but for the community to move on and see something new flourish and grow. To lead for me is to pioneer and this kind of spirit is comfortable in discovering a new path. For me, I always felt comfortable in making a new way, always wanting to learn something new. The hunger to know more is driven by the desire to always be better, and this is just part of my DNA in leading my business.

7.4.2 Developing My Team

I had the paper side of the business sorted. The business plan was written and I had support from the local Enterprise Agency in keeping me on track and helping me progress my plans. But, nothing prepared me for how to manage with staff. At the beginning I only had one employee so it was straightforward. But, as I started to grow the team, managing people became the first big struggle. As a leader, I am committed to excellence and achieving only the very best, but I was surprised by how conflict within the team was preventing my vision from becoming reality. While I am very much a computer geek and spend many hours surfing the Internet to find out new ways of doing things, in this first year of business I could find nothing to help me deal with the conflict within my team. It is one thing to lead one employee and a very different dynamic when it comes to leading six, then now as I lead fourteen members of staff. While it was a struggle at the time to solve the conflict, I came to find my authority as a leader and became comfortable in my way of managing my staff.

I found out that my way of leading was to treat my staff as colleagues, but knowing also when it matters, I am the boss and I have the final say. I would rather guide staff and show them what has to be done instead of always giving orders. To me, it is important to put myself in my staff's shoes. The balance is difficult as sometimes I connect easier with some staff more naturally than others. But, in leading I must be unbiased, and this has proved to my biggest learning curve and biggest reward. So, I make sure that my staff feel valued and part of the business. The hard work goes both ways—I am always prepared to lend a hand when needed and roll up my sleeves to support them on the ground. Some staff are part time and it can be more difficult for them to feel part of the business, so I try to get them involved in a specific project and it really brings a sense of ownership and collegiality across the team. I believe in this way, the simple things really matter, so by paying attention to the small details in the working environment my staff feel valued.

7.4.3 Rewards of Learning

I am always hungry to know more, so learning throughout my journey has been constant and I believe this has been the bedrock of my success so far. For me, it is the investment in developing my own leadership skills and ability that has proved most critical for the business. I regularly take part in networking events, seminars and programmes of learning in the local area as well as regional activities, where I get to meet and learn from more experienced business leaders and in different sectors.

I also find the webinars held by the Federation of Small Business and HMRC for example, are helpful in terms of giving me practical tips to improve the more operational aspects of the business such as in financial planning, or human resource management. However, the greatest impact of engaging in a programme of learning was Lead2Grow in 2016. I knew I needed to improve some of my leadership skills in order to grow the business to the next level. This programme was different to others because it focused on my professional and personal leadership skills and how I can manage my employees more effectively. Before the programme, my big leadership challenges were confidence, time management, delegating tasks, profitability and lack of a strategic plan for the future. It taught me the importance of looking after my own health and well-being, which gives me more energy and mental focus for running the business.

This is the biggest challenge for me leading my business is taking time to work on the business. There is always so much to do and I find sometimes I get overwhelmed with tasks to be completed. But, I know the importance of reflection and thinking about the bigger picture, so it is when I am walking or reading a book that the ideas and problem solving happens. Recently, I have found mindfulness is important routine for me. By taking time to take deep breath and be aware of my posture, I find the action of pausing, refreshing and energising. It sets me back on track. Then, it is about working with my staff to see these ideas and solutions put into practice. Communication is key to everything. I use regular staff meetings, though it can be difficult to organise as different staff work on different shifts to tell them about new learning and new projects I want to implement. How I do this is critical, so for me it is about involving the staff in the final decision-making. Even if they don't see the point in my new idea, I try and show them. This is an important dimension of the culture I try to build.

The leadership programme taught me to believe in myself as a leader and how to overcome any self doubts that the business would fail. Greater self-confidence has enabled me to train key staff in delegating smaller tasks, which in turn has reaped big rewards. In the last two years, I have received four regional and national leadership awards for best new business, best start up business and best development in enterprise, as well as Business Woman of the Year in 2016. At the time of receiving these awards, I would feel a sense of unreality, and wonder, how can this be? Then I realise in all these awards, it is the parents of the children I look after who vote for me, and that makes me feel proud of the difference I make. My next goal is to achieve an award for staff customer service. I am very proud of my staff who all go the extra mile, and I want them to be recognised for their excellence. My commitment, and the commitment of my staff to achieving excellence means the business is experiencing a significant and consistent increase in demand for childcare places to the extent that I have extended my premises and will employ two more staff to cope with the growing numbers of little hands coming my way. So in leading my business the big is most definitely in the small.

For more information on the company visit: www.articlavedaycare.com.

7.5 Aaron Mcconnell: Vynomic

Vynomic is a technology solutions company based in Northern Ireland, providing technology services and support across the region relating to outdoor, indoor, city centre Wi-Fi coverage, as well as IT networking and fault finding system recovery. Founder and owner Aaron McConnell was a research assistant for four years before he embarked on a Ph.D. at Ulster University. A few years after he graduated in 2015 he decided to embark on a new adventure by setting up his own business. Two and half years on, he tells his story of leading as a sole trader and the importance of 'pivoting' to respond to customer needs and navigate change while sustaining a trajectory of growth in the midst of hiring and firing his first two employees.

7.5.1 In the Beginning

I had graduated with a doctorate equipped with the academic knowledge in WiFi and telecommunications and technical confidence in my ability, but in 2015, I still working as a Research Associate wondering what was the next step in my career. That's when the idea happened. I

Image 7.4 Aaron McConnell

decided long range wireless connections overhead instead of ripping up roads was the solution to overcoming problems of inaccessibility to the Internet in rural locations. I also knew given the pace of technological developments, if I didn't set up my business and do it now, I would never do it. So after setting up my company Vynomic, and with continued support from Causeway Enterprise Agency, I began to offer services to the agricultural sector in Northern Ireland. But, I quickly found out that even though my product was spot on and filled a gap in the market, no one wanted to buy it. After several weeks of travelling the country, I found myself playing video games during the day, wondering what on earth was I going to do now? I kept asking myself what do farmers really want and need?

One day out of the blue, I realised that I was speaking to potential customers about my product in my language and while it was technically brilliant they didn't understand me. More importantly, I wasn't listening. My customers were telling me they wanted end-user technologies like cameras, things that would use WiFi. They weren't concerned about the fact the WiFi network allowed them to view these cameras. They only cared that it worked! They were telling me there was nothing in the market and it seemed impossible to do it, but they knew they needed it. To farmers, it was a matter of life and death for their animals and the livelihood of their business. Now, I didn't have a clue about cameras but I knew all about WiFi. So understanding the urgency to solve this problem, I went back to the drawing board and designed a new product and today Vynomic is currently the biggest camera installer for farms in Northern Ireland. I didn't plan to design and sell this product—it wasn't in my business plan, but I had to 'pivot' to make my business viable.

7.5.2 Learning to Pivot the Business

Hunger to learn is part my daily appetite. Learning for me is primarily with technology. At weekends I occasionally take an evening, sometimes until 2–3 a.m. and search for an improvement that I believe will make my business faster, safer or more profitable. With an IPad in my hand I am always looking for ways, or for items I can purchase, that will improve how some business process works. The improvements can be hit-or-miss and, if they are a hit, they often only bring marginal improvements equating to a small fraction of a percent of overall efficiency and profitability. But, nevertheless, these small changes make a bigger difference in time. At the outset I did take part in the Lead2Grow programme, which gave me insight into the importance of strategic leadership in developing the business. Today I have little time to attend business support events due to time constraints. I find business developments can happen by accident, or as the result of an unexpected event, which can be a 'forced' opportunity for improvement. I know that if do not position myself to learn then no matter the opportunity positive change will not happen if I don't take time to learn. So, for me, learning to lead is most often on the job.

Common to the growth of technological companies is the term 'pivoting'. In a nutshell, it is about reacting to market forces and supplying a different product or service to suit a more lucrative demand.

Interestingly, I discovered this strategy on Now TV by watching the series 'Silicon Valley'! My pivotal moments have come after some time away on personal trips. I occasionally take a day at the weekend to go somewhere and do something completely unrelated to the business. When I come back I tackle the issue with a whiteboard and a fresh mind where I write and rewrite notes and constantly remap my business processes to ensure relevance and improvement. My garage door is my whiteboard! Pivoting has proved critical as I found at the outset of my business when I wasn't listening to what my customers actually needed. This was the most valuable lesson I learned early in leading my business, which has become one of my mantras as I continue to lead and navigate change.

The need for pivoting was never greater when I encountered my biggest crisis to date: employing staff. A year ago, I knew for the business to grow, I needed to recruit staff. Specifically, I needed someone to install cables in a farm shed to allow me to have the time to design a new advertising campaign or develop a new service. The choice was experienced staff, who would cost more, or inexperienced staff who would cost less and could be trained. I decided to go with inexperienced staff because of the low cost, the fact they could be trained, and also because of the part subsidy by government. The plan was to develop both staff sufficiently to the point that when they completed their apprenticeships, they would be qualified network installation engineers and I could send them out to customer sites without my supervision. Initially this plan worked and both employees were keen to learn, enthusiastic about the business, and reliable. But, the situation deteriorated quickly over time to the point that up to recently, both apprentices were doing the least amount of work possible. It was a situation with a customer who viewed their poor work ethic and attitude that was the final straw and I let them go. Today I am back to square one: just me, but with a pipeline of work for more than one person to do.

I was dismayed at what happened, the risk albeit calculated resulted in double trouble. It means I am back on site with customers taking on all of the workload leaving no time for planning, calling, emailing, and developing the business. It means the ground breaking technologies I was working on have to take a backseat, again, to be worked on late at night and at weekends. But, I am back to the white board and I am pivoting the business to solve the staff problem. I have discovered Fiverr.com that provides on-demand resources for office tasks and I now outsource functions such as logo design, advertising, and administration to freelancers around the world. I have also drawn up a list of contractors who have called on me to deliver part of their contractual obligations, so I can now call on them, or on others they trust, in the same way. But, this is just a temporary fix. I know employing skilled staff is inevitable.

7.5.3 Building a Boat

Leading my business is like building a boat while I'm living on it. The boat starts off as a basic raft bound together with twine. While I know little about building boats, I know it is my leadership mission to constantly improve the boat whilst making sure I don't let it (or make it) sink in the process. Customers are like the providers of boat-building materials. Some of the materials are good and some are bad, but all are necessary. As such, the providers of materials are initially difficult to find and can be quite fickle, but strategies must be developed to find and keep them. Eventually help is required to continue work on the boat, so people are brought on board as staff. The extra weight makes the boat more likely to sink, but the hope of the leader is that despite the risk, the extra resource will make the boat better and greater. But, while I have learned growth cannot happen without the right helpers, staff will never work on your boat as hard as you will. Indeed, if your boat gets into trouble, these helpers will quickly abandon you and seek a new boat to work on.

As the leader I knows the boat must be strong enough to weather the storms that will come. Fear of a storm can mean that too much time and resources are spent on strengthening the boat in its current form, which means the boat won't get any bigger. Certainly, building too quickly from cheaper materials, can mean even a small storm might put the boat under. Herein lies the tension of developing the capacity for growth, in the right way, but also embracing the change that will always come. Making the right decision in developing the business means understanding the likely risk and the likely reward of an action or inaction. I have learned there is risk in every decision and the interpretation of risk is a factor of intelligence, experience and information. Ultimately, leadership is risk. It is about making decisions with as much knowledge as possible but at the same time understanding not all decisions will lead to the right outcomes. So, sometimes, when I have made the wrong decisions, it is the ability to 'pivot' that helps me navigate the consequences and steer the boat back on track.

7.5.4 Leading on Purpose

When I set up my business, I didn't really know why I was doing it. I used all the usual sound bites to describe my purpose 'to be successful', 'to bring new technologies to people', and 'to make the world a better place'. But, I only half-believed what I was saying. It was after a year in business I realised I was doing it because I wanted the experience of building something potentially great. There is an important distinction between wanting to build and wanting the experience of building. Some people describe their business as their child or baby, but I don't see it that way. I have gained significant experience of getting this far with my business and that is important to me. I have developed new knowledge, new expertise and gained new wisdom I would not have in any other way. If this company fails despite my best efforts, then I believe the experience of building will help me build another business, but greater. This is why mistakes don't terrify me, or torture me after I've made them.

The business has flourished to a point that I am continuing to provide WiF cameras to the farming market, and at the same time delivering high-speed WiFi in town centres, primary schools, and businesses using renewable energy and without digging up the earth or erecting large masts. Development of the technology has matured to a point that international markets are the next step as I seek opportunities to provide high speed Internet access to rural communities in the developing world. But, life is finite. I have decided in my mid-30s, this is my best chance of building a business and experience the ups and downs while working towards something great. Getting rich was never part of my motivation and purpose. Even now, as my turnover is more than doubling year on year, I view the extra income as the opportunity to do build the boat, to enable the next extension or rebuild an existing business process so that the business is leaner and more fruitful. I take less than the minimum wage home and spend less than fifty pounds per month on non-essentials or myself. I know profit is pleasant and necessary but it is only the secondary goal. My core focus is on gaining the experience of developing something great.

For more information on the company visit: www.vynomic.com.

7.6 Chapter Summary

The stories in this chapter point out that the effective combination of entrepreneurial leadership skills can flourish in a wide range of enterprises and industries, from childcare to surf board manufacturing. Each small business leader in telling their story demonstrates key entrepreneurial leadership skills such as opportunity seeking, achievement striving, risk bearing, and proactive behaviour. Above all, they each display a deep sense of purpose in doing business and life. The nurture of staff in building their team, their passionate productivity while living out values and principles on a daily basis that form the key dimensions of their leadership priorities. But, it is the ability to thrive in uncertainty is what sets these entrepreneurial leaders apart from the many small firms who fail in the first five years of business. The next chapter of each story has yet to be written and there is no doubt each leader is excited about what lies ahead.

8

Storytelling: 10 Years On

Abstract The stories from entrepreneurial leaders who have successfully navigated the challenges of business for more than ten years provide critical insight into the longer journey of leadership as well as the lessons learned along the way. A diverse portfolio of stories are told by business leaders operating in a wide range of sectors from environmental waste solutions to coffee, medical production to business support services. There is no doubt that while the challenges may differ at a local level, the common traits of leadership purpose met with the capacity to consistently embrace and manage change underpins the success of each business in this chapter.

Keywords Storytelling · Entrepreneurial leaders · Leadership development · Purpose · Learning to lead · Metaphorical expression Lessons learned · Business support agency · Medical production Environmental solutions · Coffee

8.1 Introduction

There is a lack of academic understanding of what constitutes leadership in the context of the small business organisation. To this end, the current chapter presents the stories of entrepreneurial leaders of growing small and medium sized companies in the UK. Entrepreneurial leadership is most often associated with the leaders of new ventures, as told in chapter seven in this book. But, the stories herein provide evidence of entrepreneurial leadership that has stood the test of time flourishing in a wide range of sectors. Each leader remembers the small beginnings of their story and describes the highs and the lows of the journey thus far. In all the stories told, there is no doubt that regardless of the external incentives used to help the business grow, without the ambition, drive and energy by the leader to make it happen, the ending of the story would have been very different. As in the previous chapter of stories, metaphorical expression is likewise used to bring the narratives of entrepreneurial leadership to life.

8.2 Jayne Taggart: Causeway Enterprise Agency

The Causeway Enterprise Agency (CEA) was established in 1984 as a local business support organisation, providing quality start up support for fledging entrepreneurs in Northern Ireland. For over 30 years, as a lead anchor institution in the Causeway Coast region, CEA has significant experience of workforce development and meeting the needs of start-up and small firms. Jayne Taggart, who was appointed as CEO ten years ago, tells her story of developing her small but talented and committed team with a vibrant board of directors in the midst of significant changes to public sector funding. Growing from two to five business parks, Jayne explains the lessons learned in how to deal with the constant change in the market place and how to pursue the right opportunities to develop the organisation. One of the many achievements was securing UKCES funding in 2015 and working with the author on the planning and project management of the Lead2Grow micro business leadership programme. The organisation has made a significant impact in the local economy evidenced by a contribution of £25 million to the local economy and the creation of almost 7000 jobs. Their success has been recognised through a number of high profile awards including the prestigious Queens Award for Enterprise secured in 2014 in recognition of service and contribution to enterprise.

8.2.1 Master Gardener

Ten years ago I stepped up to the role of CEO inheriting a team of six employees and a 50,000 square feet incubation space accommodating over 26 tenant companies. I had learned the craft of supporting entrepreneurs in a previous role in the organisation, but as CEO I was provided with a bigger opportunity to make a bigger economic and social impact in my local community. I have lived in this area all my life, so it was important to me I played my part in making it a better place to live, educate, work and do business. I use the analogy of the master gardener to reflect my approach in leading the team at CEA. Indeed, I can liken my role at CEA to that of the master gardener in that it is my job to plan out how much of the landscape should be devoted to different plant varieties, as well as how much shade or how much sun is needed to provide every business has the best chance of success. I am constantly tending the garden, checking the conditions of the soil to safeguard the right environment for the entrepreneur and create a thriving and vibrant garden. But, my job is to also work with more mature businesses, which provide another level of shelter and support in the garden. The mentoring and presence of longer established entrepreneurs gives the garden a sense of maturity and profile. While gardeners put much time, effort and love into caring for their plants, in the end I know that the final results aren't completely in my control. In the end, it is the entrepreneur who will ultimately determine the success of the new business.

The scale and geographical dispersion of the organisation across five sites, as well as the management of a new social enterprise, requires strategic leadership embedded in deep collaboration with the CEA team.

It is a joined up approach whereby together we create an environment of shared passion and commitment as a foundation for the development, growth, creativity and success of small businesses as well as our organisation. For me it has been about developing a high performance team empowered to listen to the entrepreneur, wrap around the relevant support package, and lead them on a journey from research informed planning to official start-up. The board of directors is another critical dimension to the CEA team, made up of civic leaders in the region from Managing Directors of SMEs and micro firms, as well as representation from the local University. Together our mission is to serve small business owners, whether new or more established, helping most of all to build confidence and a strength of ambition to succeed and grow. While I stick my fingers in the dirt from time to time to make adjustments and check if the process needs more water, it is important to resist the temptation to micro manage. I appreciate plants will not grow if I keep tugging them out of the ground to check the roots.

8.2.2 Gardening in a Crisis

I have enjoyed the fruits of my labour to date with a strong track record of positive and real economic impact in terms of new start-ups, improved survival rate, and job creation. Most notable for me was the Queens Award for Enterprise in 2014 in recognition of my recognition of service and contribution to enterprise. This allowed me to take a breath and then keep going to drive the next stage of growth for the organisation, which has included a new social enterprise in the creative industry sector, the take over of two more business parks and the development of a bespoke leadership programme for micro leaders called Lead2Grow. But, the journey has not always been straightforward. One of the most significant challenges I faced was in 2011 and 2012, when the organisation lost the contract to deliver the country's Business Start Programme. Prior to this we had enjoyed the privilege of sole delivery agent for the Borough for over 25 years. We were the first port of call for any entrepreneur seeking to start a new business, so the whole identity and purpose of the organisation was built around this programme.

All of a sudden the tables had turned and the organisation was no longer in possession of its core brand.

This crisis marks a significant shift in my learning as CEO. It was a huge shock. I can see now how initially I didn't handle the news well. It was a case of flight or fight, and I chose to fight. The result was internal stress within my team and the organisation, as well as negative stakeholder relations externally. The reality was a huge sea change in government funding and this crisis was only the beginning of more public sector cuts and fundamental changes to the operation of LEAs (Local Enterprise Agencies). So, I quickly learned the better response was to regroup as an organisation and with help from the Board of Directors we spent some time working on a strategy to develop a new operating model that would enable us to operate without government funding. Change outside our control is constant, so my strategy now is to view each problem as an opportunity for the organisation to do something different. After this, we continued to support entrepreneurs in our region by developing our own interventions and support programmes and 12 months later the contract was back within our remit. But by operating a new business model we have put in place a number of strategies around support in our local communities that is self-funding providing the organisation with a sustainable future.

It can be a lonely place as a CEO and this crisis also demonstrated the need for me to access learning and support as part of my leadership development. Earlier in my leadership career I was not very good at carving out the time to take part in skills development of programmes of learning. I often found such programmes too content heavy, with a classroom lecture style and overall irrelevant to me as the leader of a business support organisation. But, since the crisis, I have actively sought learning and development in different ways, through mentoring, peer learning and networking. Not only have I learned from the mentoring provided by my former Chairmen of the board, my active involvement with the Enterprise Northern Ireland Board, where I sit around the table with other CEO's of LEAs, allows me to share experiences and learning with my peers. I also find I am unconsciously learning though local CEA networking events and workshops. This exposure to new ideas and creative solutions, and listening to the lessons learned from other leaders in a wide range of organisations, keeps me relevant to the market place of new and small businesses. So in an ever-changing environment, the willingness to always learn is an important attitude that keeps my pencil sharp in making sure I make the right and informed decisions on a daily basis.

8.2.3 Survival Seeds

The focus of CEA, as indeed most LEAs has been business support for new start ups, providing a wide range of services in business planning, finance, marketing, networking events and general entrepreneurial skills development. Leading the delivery of business support to over 1400 new start-ups in the last ten years, I could see that the difference between the survival and failure of a new business was the owner, regardless of the challenges internally or in the external market. It is true, of course that every small business is unique in many ways, but I think in certain fundamental ways, every small business share similar challenges and traits. In my experience of working with start-ups in the first five years of leading their new business, I can identify five key attributes and skills of the owner that enables success:

1. Self awareness: the sense of the business owner knowing who they are, the good and the bad and what is needed to the bridge the gap. This builds the capacity to make informed decisions and to enable improved performance of the leader and the business.
2. Passion, commitment and drive: without these ingredients, others will not see what the leader sees in their business. This is the ingredient that helps the leader stay the course in the midst of significant challenges in the marketplace.
3. Ability to collaborate and build relationships: for some business owners there is a natural propensity to network and collaborate, but for others this critical aspect of doing and building business is not in their DNA. But, this is a critical skill for building, empowering and engaging internally with employees, as well as connecting and understanding the needs and wants of customers.

4. Agility and adaptability: now more than ever, it is the willingness of the business owner to stay open to new ideas, adapt to new situations, and then manage the change in a positive manner, that enables long-term success. Indeed, it is listening carefully to the signs and then being able to quickly respond with the right solution or strategy that is most pertinent in doing business today.
5. Plan for success: business leaders, especially in the early days must be equipped with the self-belief that they can and will make the business succeed. From this positive posture of heart and mind, the leader must set the goals and develop the strategy to deliver the success of the business.

I can clearly identify the critical skills and qualities of small business leaders, but I know not all entrepreneurs have natural ability in these areas. I also understand the mainstream provision of leadership development programmes is not relevant in terms of the context of the learning and the issues encountered in new and very small businesses. A conversation with the author became the seed of a new idea and we secured government funding for a pilot leadership programme specifically designed for the owners of micro firms, which then led to a wider programme with funding from the UKCES. We had to rethink the traditional viewpoint of leader as hero and incorporate a distributed leadership model in an entrepreneurial context focused on culture, empowerment, knowledge sharing and building talent. The impact in terms of the improved performance and growth for our local small business leaders was more than we ever predicted, which for CEA provides a strong business case going forward in securing future support for leadership development with the micro business sector.

As master gardener, I have the responsibility of sowing the seeds of survival for start-ups and small businesses in my local community. Over the last ten years I have watched the harvest reap in almost 1500 new start-ups in the Causeway Coast and Glens region. I have enjoyed success in the improved performance and development of our local small business leaders making a notable contribution to economic growth through job creation. There is no doubt fundamental changes in the climate are impacting upon the structure of the garden. Nonetheless, my purpose remains absolute. I will continue to provide a real and meaningful connection with small business leaders in my community that nurtures inspiration, self-belief and motivation so these firms can achieve their true potential.

Image 8.1 Jayne Taggart

8.3 John Armstrong: Armstrong Medical

In 1984 John Armstrong started out in business working from his garage selling medical disposable products. Since then, Armstrong Medical has grown considerably to become a worldwide leading manufacturer and supplier of high quality, innovative respiratory disposables for anesthesia and critical care. From humble beginnings manufacturing medical disposables from Causeway Enterprise Agency, Armstrong Medical now operates from a 90,000 square foot office, warehouse and manufacturing facility with over 130 employees. The Company's manufacturing resources include state of the art automated tubing extrusion and robotic injection moulding; class 10,000 and 100,000 type clean rooms; and bespoke assembly with research and development facilities. In the field of acute respiratory care this medium-sized business based in Northern Ireland is setting the standard with a global reputation for developing high quality, innovative products. John shares over thirty years of experience growing the business on a global scale operating in over 60 countries worldwide. This has been recognised by the highly prestigious Queen's Award for International Trade and Enterprise. His story also tells the tale of leading through crisis and the lessons learned in managing change throughout the journey.

8.3.1 Creating Support for Life

I was a medical representative for five years and was frustrated with the lack of new products my employer at that time was developing. In the 1980s (as it is today), the healthcare sector was under severe pressure and in desperate need for new solutions. Equipped with working knowledge of the healthcare market, but no medical qualifications, I knew there was a gap in the market. From the increasing demands on valuable nursing time, to the wrestling with diminishing budgets by clinicians under pressure to provide the best patient care, hospitals were required to cut down on the number of failed therapies. But, for me it was about more than health economics. 'Creating support for Life' was the purpose from the outset and over 30 years later it is still the personal motivation for me as well as the core mission of the Company. What we do is more than selling pieces of plastic to make a profit. Most of all I am proud of the fact our products can make a real and positive difference to a patient's quality of life.

This mission is motivated both by my personal ambition as well as the Company's values to be creative, supportive, and live life. As my Company's aim is to make a difference to the quality of life of hospital patients, I am aware that one day Armstrong Medical products could save the life of someone in my family or even myself. When one of my first potential customers said 'come back in three years if you are still in business', I was determined to make sure the business succeeded. We have experienced a challenging but rewarding journey thus far, but a recent case has served to underscore the reality of our sense of purpose. One of our sales staff was in a hospital demonstrating our products when a cancer patient in their final hours became very distressed. Struggling to breath the doctor applied our CPAP system and it offered immediate relief enabling the patient to spend their last hours talking and writing a letter to their loved ones. I will never know how many lives we have saved or how many patients have experienced better quality of life and outcome, but bottom line, I know without a doubt, we have made a difference. In business, that is something that inspires us.

8.3.2 The Illusion of Paradise

Developing the business is somewhat like sailing for that ideal paradise island on the horizon called 'Turnover and Profit'. Giving up the comfort of a full-time job, salary, company car and all expenses, I was nevertheless excited as I began the Armstrong Medical journey, working from my garage while my wife took on a new job to make ends meet. Looking back I set out on the journey filled with an abundance of hope, more than a drop of resilience, fuelled by a stable home life, and determined to make my business successful. In the early days I had to steer my boat around and through storms such as finance, banks and cash flow. Under-currents in the water such as rising expenses, staff issues, and the downward spiral of market prices made it difficult at times to gain headway. There were even times when I had to navigate the shark infested waters of patents, product issues, regulatory, legal and process issues and dare I say it business consultants, only to realise when I eventually made a way through, it was like there was a barrier reef consisting of competition and supply chain issues just under the waterline threatening our very survival.

In the first two years the Company did not make any profit. In reality, it took us to the third year to break even. When we reached the four year point, we started to gather a small profit on that so called island of paradise, but quickly discovered what looked like beautiful golden sands were populated by flocks of seabirds in the form of HR issues, recruitment, retention of staff and all the related challenges that comes with growing the team. Time to move on again. The next stage of the journey for the Company was to find a new island, which for us was manufacturing. But, guess what? We encountered similar challenges albeit with a different set of problems along the way. Now with a turnover of over £11.5 million and employing 130 staff, some would say we have reached that Special Place, but the reality is we are small fry in comparison to the global corporate giants in the world of medical device manufacturing. The global reputation of our Company has grown from our ability and expertise in designing innovative products with patient safety to the foreground at all times. It has been this commitment to innovation (which requires managing change on a constant basis) that allows us to compete in an uneven playing field with a high quality and differentiated customer service.

8.3.3 Refiners Fire

In 2007, our factory went on fire, which overnight wiped out 90% of our manufacturing, all of our computers, systems, administration and production processes, and caused £6 million worth of damage. The next morning I had to make a decision to rebuild or retreat. I decided the former and led a small group of people with the task to rebuild the business, which was in reality a daily hand to mouth process. We were forced to forget excellence in product production and hope our customers would be gracious enough to accept our products until we could get back to full manufacturing capability. We had no idea how we could continue to manufacture and supply our products, but nonetheless we asked our customers to keep giving us orders. Somehow we were able to honour each order made. But, flexibility was everything. Experience taught us that decisions made at 9 am could change at 12 noon in order to prioritise another urgent order. Most of all, I learned the strength of clear decision-making from myself in leading the business from the onset of the crisis, this had the critical influence in galvanising the rest of my employees into action. I had to keep moving forward not having all the answers, but learning to lead in the moment and with an imperfect and sometimes very foggy plan.

We did learn about the "Sound of Silence". As a business we were left to figure out a way forward on our own without any professional assistance. But, the kindness of the community extending help and support in many different ways willed us to recover. Moreover, it was the graciousness of our customers that kept the orders and the money coming in. The fire as a critical event was one thing, but the recovery period was another. The resilience of staff was so important and recognising staff fatigue became critical to survival, we got to understand that making sure the "Good News" stories were told, became the oxygen of the business as we rebuilt literally from the ashes. Overall I was left with a realisation that people look for and need leadership not only in a crisis, but also in everyday life. It is part of the fabric of our human being. The truth is, the Company grew more the year after the fire than it had done before or since. I can't fully explain that, it certainly makes me wonder. Not long after the crisis, we received the highly prestigious Queen's Award for International Trade and Enterprise in 2009 as a result of our growth in our distribution network worldwide.

8.3.4 Changing Gear

Five years after the fire, in spite of our best efforts, the Company had plateaued in terms of sales. We were working hard but making no headway and at this point in the history of the business I formed a new and valuable understanding of complacency. The subliminal cancer of complacency tried to threaten our future survival. Looking back, I can see this was partly the result of staff fatigue and relief from surviving the fire. But, complacency in staff is one of the greatest challenges I have encountered as Managing Director. I would have said we had good staff but complacency is an unaware condition we drift into. I was left with little choice but to embark on a culture change throughout the Company. I have found that stimulation is the antidote to complacency. This has been the greatest change project I have led to date, which has involved staff from the board room to the cleaners, in a wide range of activities including the stimulation of new schemes, investment in new staff and equipment, training and education of existing staff, product development, LEAN manufacturing, clinical engagement, communication skills development, strategy days, redevelopment of Vision and Values, mentoring programs and best practice visits to other companies.

Kaizen is the Japanese word for 'change for good' and typifies the most efficient way a group of people can work together through a change process in manufacturing, assembly or administration contexts. Prioritising urgency as top of the list for change, we adopted the principles of Kaizen across all parts of the business, which has reaped big rewards in terms of improvement to the bottom line. One of the best books I have read has been Professor John Kotter's fable "Our Iceberg is melting". It became my blueprint in how to lead change in my business and for good. I have learned that while the Company can embark on in-house teaching and education (which is so important), in our case most learning actually takes place in the reality of the hospital. Acknowledging the importance of the principles of this simplistic fable, led to us identifying our own group of Squidfishers in the Company who go looking for fresh fishing grounds and new icebergs in the medical world. In our case it's new and better ways of doing things, new markets and opportunities, new product development etc. They proudly wear the penguin badge I awarded to them recently at all meetings.

Throughout the journey I can see looking back that change was indeed a constant. A few years ago, I had to admit I needed help to change gear and move the business forward. Like many leaders in business, I didn't go to University nor have achieved any recognised formal business management qualifications so I decided to become part of a regional network 'Vistage'. This is a fee paying membership organisation for Chief Executives and Managing Directors who take a day a month to be together to discuss the real time issues and challenges of running a profitable business. The investment of time and money into this group has taught me that quiet thinking time is of the utmost importance in making balanced decisions in business and keeping everything in perspective. Taking time out is one of the most challenging parts of leading as the busyness of the day to day can take over. Presently, I am in the process of leading another change management project for the company as I put in place a succession plan for the future. So, in moving forward I know there will be further challenges waiting just around the corner.

Image 8.2 John Armstrong

8.4 Mark Mckinney: ATG Group

Dr. Mark McKinney formed the ATG Group in 2006, an environmental and waste solutions company based in Northern Ireland. Starting in a home office the company has achieved significant growth year on year operating today with five offices throughout Ireland, the UK and worldwide. The company deals with a wide range of environmental and waste issues, providing tailored solutions such as remediation technology for redundant sites, invasive plant species eradication, spill control products, and environmental training programmes for both public and private sector clients. With over 18 years experience in the remediation industry, Mark tells his story of leading ATG to become a market leader with 80% of their business today outside Northern Ireland. About to double their staff numbers, the company is embarking on further global expansion plans in Kuwait, Africa and the Baltic States. Mark explains his dedication not only to developing new and innovative technology, but investing in people to ensure sustainable growth. This story is also about community values and giving others a 'Second Chance', the name of the company's charity.

8.4.1 Dream and a Prayer

It all started with a dream and a prayer. I had a beautiful home shared with my wife, our two children and together we lived a very privileged life. But, a spiritual encounter in September 2004 was the beginning of a significant period of transformation in our lives. The dream of ashes to gold about a large successful global company was one thing, but it was the subsequent prayer that sparked a new journey of highs and lows for my family and me. I had to go back to basics. I had to sell my big car, downsize my house, leave my well-paid job and simplify my lifestyle in preparation. But, I wasn't prepared for the fact I had to wait a year before the adventure started. Anyone can plan around a dream, but putting it into action was the real challenge. Turning the dream into reality doesn't happen overnight and it comes with a cost, but there is no doubt in looking back the journey thus far is worth it.

The establishment of ATG (which represents Air, Terrain and Ground Water contamination issues, as well Ashes to Gold), started with me, myself and I working in my garage. In the beginning, it was simple and small, but supported by the Causeway Enterprise Agency and Invest NI, I was able to chart a way forward to grow my business. Although while it is necessary to write a business plan, I found it never mirrors the reality of doing business or prepares you for the unexpected. In the first few years, the business developed slowly and steadily, but I was determined to expand according to the cash flow to ensure we did not accrue any debt, especially during the recession. Even as the pace of growth has quickened in the last two years, the original dream, along side my wife, has anchored me in leading the company in the right way. This has kept me focused on staying true to the values of the company to seek out the gold across the business from recruiting new staff, to managing our existing team, as well as pursuing new business opportunities.

8.4.2 In the 'Fishing' Business

As far back as I can remember I have always loved water. For whatever reason, water is fundamental to who I am. So much so, I find the best place to think, reflect and strategise is with water, either in it or close by it. It transports me back to my childhood and adolescent years to a special time when my life was consumed with a passion for fishing. Captain of the school fishing team my role was always to analyse the water, the pegs, and the bait in order to develop a strategy that would quite literally blow the competition out of the water. Under instruction from my teacher, I learned about the patterns of fishing, what different species like to eat, where they would hide, where they would be at different times of the day, and how to find them. Against the odds (I went to a school not far from the bottom of the education league table!) we went on to win a series of regional competitions and the Ulster Schools fishing completion twice in four years.

Today, I can see that fishing is still a passion, albeit on land and in the world of business. From the analytical skills critical for scanning the environment and developing the strategic direction of the business, to the importance of mentoring from experts in the field, the story is the same. I learned the importance of seasons and timing in fishing, which has proved an essential lesson in the waiting and wondering in my journey of leading ATG. Most of all, I love to fish for human potential. Not always the obvious individuals, but those who fit our culture with the potential to grow and develop. Essentially, I look for people who can replace me and are better than me at things I am not good at. My strategy has always been to coach and invest in my staff to bring out the gold. I take them to the point where I can see they are trained and ready for the next step and when they least expect it, I throw them in the deep end. They all learn the art of swimming then!

The heart of the business has been to build an atmosphere of hard working individuals working as an effective team to bring about a great customer experience and an innovative approaches to problem solving while making a profit (which is shared with the staff). But, as in fishing, there is always one who got away. For me one of the biggest crisis points I have encountered was loosing a vital member of my team, my succession plan for the business. Up until then, I always had the ability to see when people had to leave, making their departure a healthy and positive event for them and the business. But, this time, I had mentored one of my senior team for nine years to replace me. He had all the qualities and values I sought in a Managing Director for my company- honesty, integrity, processing skills, respect and rapport with staff. But, when he announced he was leaving, it was a huge shock. I learned I couldn't control other people's decisions even when it was painful, I had choose to see the gold.

8.4.3 Giving a Second Chance

Advice from my Grandfather told me 'turnover is vanity and profit is sanity' and there is no doubt of the wisdom in these words. While profit is necessary to grow and succeed, for ATG this is not our sole purpose. It was important to me, as part of the 'ashes to gold' dream, that I build a strong and profitable base for the company so we can reinvest some of that back into the community. Motivated by the desire to rebuild, restore and transform my local community, I set up the charity Second Chance where we invest 10% of the company's net profits. I want to see a community that is thriving and sustained in helping and empowering others to be rebuilt, restored and transformed. My mum was my biggest supporter and always believed in me, even when I didn't believe in me. Her values of generosity and kindness have always inspired me. So, bottom line, I want to do the same and create a new story for people who really need a break. The charity supports over 150 people through apprenticeship schemes for the long-term unemployed, learning disabilities, providing help in areas of physical and mental health and meaningful activities to help these people find purpose and grow in confidence.

So, to make this happen on the ground, we employ two full-time and two part-time employees in our high street shop that sells clothes and accessories, as well as up cycled furniture and a small café area. Second Chance receives donations of unwanted, pre-owned household items, which are cleaned, repaired, up-cycled or recycled, and then sold in our shop. The approach taken is unique in that it offers the individuals who volunteer in the centre the opportunity to increase their confidence, motivation and self-belief while learning new skills. We hope this help them gain employment in the future and ultimately improve their quality of life, giving them a much-needed "2nd chance". A recent development for the charity has seen the establishment of a social enterprise called Avodah bake house, which supports a local baker and entrepreneur in fulfilling his dream. But, for me the giving back doesn't stop here. I would like to see more dreams come true not just in the local community but across the world, so it is my goal to see this end of the business continue to grow and evolve to give many others a second chance.

8.4.4 'We Are Going to Need a Bigger Boat….' (Jaws, 1975)

At present, we are a small specialist company with strong credentials, customer retention, and a track record of repeat business. We operate in a competitive market with other providers offering a similar portfolio of environmental treatment and remediation services. However, we are recognised as innovators and often find competitors imitating and attempting to copy our treatments. I have learned there is really no single thing that will provide a distinctive competitive advantage, but rather it will come from the combination and totality of a number of service elements, together with a commitment to customer-service excellence and responsiveness. So while a small company, developments in R&D enable us to play the game with the big players in our industry.

Prestigious projects are also important to us in terms of PR and get people talking about the company.

In order to see the next stage of the dream come true, we need to build a bigger boat (as said in the famous Jaws movie in 1975). So enlisting support from Invest NI, I have help for the company in two key ways, technological innovation and staff development. Our vision and strategic objectives for the business are for growth through extending firstly our geographic reach with the extension of our domestic market presence into Great Britain and the Republic of Ireland and then expanding our overseas activities in Europe and Africa. This will involve further expansion of our range of services and add new proprietary technology/products with an annual £250,000 spend on R&D. We are looking to make a £1.6 million investment in the next 6 weeks to further extend our reach and services into the UK market with a hazardous waste treatment facility to be purchased in Scotland which has a license to treat 135,000 tons a year of waste on a 6 acre site.

However, money is just one aspect necessary to make it happen. Our immediate key growth issues are simply, but significantly, marketing bandwidth and resources, recruiting suitable technical staff and improving our internal processes and IT infrastructure. But, I recognise my staff are the company's greatest asset, critical to overcoming the challenges that lie ahead and achieving our dream. We have already started growing the business with the recruitment of a new project director, commercial manager, in country operations manager, and IT Manager. Nonetheless, with a relatively young management team at present, I am putting in place management development strategies for each staff to ensure retention and succession planning with Invest NI and the Northern Ireland Leader programme. Both plans for increasing our staff team and the R&D side of the business, means we have out grown our current buildings, so part of the next stage in the journey is the move to new large premises to grow the base for the establishment of a greater overseas presence. The next decision will be our acquisition strategy and we are currently working on a model that will enable this to happen without risking the core business. I look forward to exciting days with a vision to build the ATG Group into a PLC over the next 5 years, so watch this space.

Image 8.3 Mark McKinney

For more information on the company visit www.atg-group.co.uk.

8.5 Karen Gardiner: Ground Espresso Bars

Ground Espresso Bars Ltd is a family owned and independently operated coffee business, established in 2001. A graduate in food and environmental science, Karen Gardiner has always been passionate about local high quality food and the environment, but most of all she loved a challenge. While Karen and her husband owned four businesses before Ground was born, it was this company that has proved both the greatest challenge and greatest reward. In 2001 there were no multinational coffee chains in Northern Ireland, so artisan coffee was a new concept to consumers in the local community. The ambition to become the only chain of coffee bars in Northern Ireland with excellent artisan coffee came to pass only a few years after starting the business. Today, Ground is the largest independent coffee shop in the region employing over two hundred staff with 19 stores in North and South of Ireland, with plans to expand into the GB market. In this story, Karen also describes a deeper purpose that drives her need for success. She explains how ethical sourcing has always been important to her, but how the financial success of Ground has enabled the company to deliver real community impact in South America.

8.5.1 Challenge-Driven

I was a job hopper. For several years after my degree I quickly got bored when a job failed to challenge me. My husband and I owned four different businesses before we started Ground and while each one paid the bills, there was no excitement or passion there to sustain my commitment. Ground Espresso was born out of my need to work in a local business that would give me flexibility, as I just had my first child. With a background in catering (one of my earlier businesses was a high-end catering business) I foolishly thought this venture would be easy. We joined forces with a good friend in the new business venture, but soon realised coffee was something of a dark art. In 2001 there were no multinational coffee chains in Northern Ireland. Even though most local consumers didn't even know what an espresso was, I knew I didn't want to serve cheap and nasty coffee. I hadn't a clue what I was doing so driven by the desire to make sure it was right, I spent a lot of time at the beginning with a roasting company in Glasgow. But, all the R&D in the world couldn't have prepared us for our critics. Most of our customers just wanted a milky coffee, boiled to an inch of its life, so trying to educate our local customers was a considerable challenge.

In the first two years of business there was no boredom at all. Indeed, there were many times at the beginning I thought we had ventured down the wrong path. It was a steep and constant learning curve all about survival, yet I thrived in the midst of it all. A number of crisis points in the early journey almost proved fatal for the business. Opening our second store was a disaster. In the first 6 months they closed the road with no public access, which prevented customer access to the shop. Once the road re-opened, we appointed a new manager, who after two months fled to a new country with a substantial amount of our money. We had bear the full cost wiping out all of our reserves. It was year five before we got back on our feet again and at this point we bought out our original business partner. We knew then we were really on our own and we had to make it work for the sake of our family and our staff. Opening our third store was the turning point for us and we became energised once again. We now owned our own mini chain of Ground coffee shops, so all the dreaming and hard work was starting to pay off.

8.5.2 Building a Fleet

The phrase '*a skilled mariner was never made in a calm sea*' rings true for my journey in leading and growing Ground. In my experience, sometimes I have to do a whole lot of things wrong before I get it right, and setting up four businesses before Ground is testimony to this learning. When we started to build our fleet of Ground ships, I was scared each time one went out to sea for the first time. While ships are safe in the harbor, I know it is not what ships were built for, so for me it has been about embracing the risk and potential dangers, to drive growth. We have 19 ships now and have recruited first class captains who take charge of each store. It can be plain sailing for weeks, but then there are times when it feels like our 19 ships are in deep troubled waters and I need to call the coast guard. Some say, till the ship stays course and sails in fair weather, the captain's effort goes unnoticed, but hit the first giant wave, and his/her leadership is in the spotlight. For this has rung true, but the storms come and go. In between, it is about putting in place the right people trained for the job, as well as the right structures and processes to enable survival.

It was the decision to build our third ship in the fleet that forced me to review my leadership role in driving the company's growth. My husband was focused on running our other company in a very different sector, so the management of daily operations in all of our stores was my primary responsibility. I knew growing from three to four stores meant I couldn't carry on performing both strategic and operational tasks, especially when my own family was growing. The best decision I ever made for both Ground and my family was to work 'on' the business not 'in' it. When I stepped out of the daily running of the stores I didn't take a wage as I felt it couldn't be justified. Despite initial negativity from staff, within a few weeks of meeting suppliers I changed the distribution network and saved the company £20,000. This was not just a turning point in leading the business, but I discovered securing a good deal was a new dimension to my challenge driven motivation.

8.5.3 Charting New Waters

It has always been a husband-wife team leading Ground, making the big decisions to grow together. As a result of the success of the strong brand ethos of Ground has created new opportunities for us to collaborate with multinational retailers in the local and GB market. In the last few years we partnered with NEXT and Waterstones and Tesco to establish a new type of Ground coffee shop within a larger store. At the same time we were growing the company we were growing our family, which presented a different set of challenges. Every time I left the business to have a baby, I watched how the financial figures would change and not in a positive way. I realised even though the store managers were looking after their own store, no one was driving the performance of the managers. Only because the business was financially robust at this time, did it not evolve into a crisis. In returning from maternity seven years ago, I understood it was time to put in place more formal processes and structures, but I didn't know how.

The requests from retailers were coming in thick and fast. I could see the fleet had expanded to a point where we needed new knowledge and capability to meet this demand. But, I struggled to see how we could balance the need to devolve power across stores while at the same time keeping control of the company. The expertise was not in-house so we embarked on a partnership with the local University to develop a business growth strategy for expansion nationwide. This work enabled us to develop a new infrastructure aligned to our vision and ethos with formal processes to improve efficiency and effectiveness critical for meeting customer needs. In order to sustain the company's long-term strategic development, we made several appointments to our new senior team to alleviate the workload. This included a new regional manager, who was able to be out in our stores reviewing the business and the processes, leaving working on the set up of new stores and products to me. The added value for us has been the sharing of the management burden. Particularly, in providing unbiased support when we need it most; in some cases telling us all will be ok and the ships will stay afloat, while we get the next fleet of Ground ships ready for opening.

8.5.4 Drinking an Ethical Cup of Coffee

It is amazing to me to watch the fundamental shift in consumer behaviour with regard to coffee drinking over the last 16 years, now a global phenomenon. I have witnessed how coffee has become more than just a 'morning fix' but a national pastime and social event, contributing to employment and the economy at a local, national and global level. It is evident in the provincial towns were we have Ground stores that the increased growth in coffee shops and particularly multinational chains defies the widespread concern over other vacancy rates. There is no doubt we have enjoyed the benefits of this trend, but the purpose in growing the company is not solely motivated by profit. Ethical sourcing has always been very important to the company and me. Tracing my passion for issues relating to the natural world, global ethics, and environmental issues comes from my student days when I studied environmental biology. But from the outset, we chose our coffee roaster based on their ethical values and passion, as the leading roaster of sustainable coffee in the UK and Ireland with nearly 90% of their volume as Fairtrade.

From an early point in the business, I could see sadly that turnover wouldn't fall if I purchased unethical coffee. Unfortunately most customers don't care enough to let it affect where they go for coffee. But, it mattered to me, my family and therefore Ground, and that was enough. So, as the company has grown, so does our commitment to people and the planet. We strive to partner with suppliers and employees who uphold our values of integrity, responsibility, kindness, and innovation. The greater why for me in ethical sourcing is important in two ways. Firstly, as a company we purposively select our coffee blend origins to tie in with the co-operatives who are doing great work around the world in the 'coffee belt'.

Secondly, linked to this, in the last two years we have worked on a series of community education projects in a co-operative called Capucas in Honduras. We were involved in the creation and the building of a local community education and IT school with an university access point. When we met the children and teachers we see the appreciation as well as the tangible impact upon the potential of their education and future. It is only then I understand my business has fulfilled its purpose. The past two years on this project have brought me huge personal satisfaction and joy, more than any extra amount of money in my bank account ever could. But, this difference is only made possible as a result of the financial success of Ground and our brand. So this has become my key motivation now to ensure we are a profitable business with the ability to continue to support local communities in the coffee growing regions where our beans come from. I not only love that there is a Ground legacy out there in the world for my family and myself, but that there is also no doubt these visits to origin and spending time in these communities keeps our passion alive and our feet well and truly grounded (forgive the pun).

Image 8.4 Karen Gardiner

For more information on the company visit: www.groundcoffee.net

8.6 Chapter Summary

This chapter has provided evidence of high impact entrepreneurs that lead businesses with above average results in terms of job creation, wealth creation, and the fact they can be defined as entrepreneurial role models. It is evident that what sets these entrepreneurial leaders apart from other small business leaders is their ambition to grow, as well as the confidence and capability to make it happen, despite unpredictability in their environment. Moreover, it can be argued the combination of leadership and entrepreneurship skills positively related to strategy formulation, responsiveness and overcoming barriers to growth are the fundamental drivers of performance. As presented in Chap. 6, there is no doubt from the stories told by these entrepreneurial leaders, to lead well is to learn continually.

9
Conclusion

Abstract This chapter marks not the end of the discussion, but rather provides a synopsis of the plot and the main character in the story of leading small business. In doing so, it provides a synopsis of the main themes bringing together the insights from each chapter. To lead is to learn, so attention is given to the core lessons from the research undertaken and the stories told by the entrepreneurial leaders in the book in the form of five home truths. With a final call to action, the chapter will outline a number of key recommendations for future research and support of small business leadership.

Keywords Small business · Leadership · Power of stories · Plot of story Main character · Call to action

9.1 Plot of Story

The research and writing for this book was a four year journey in developing a narrative of leading small business. Not an exclusive story per se, but an untold one. A story worthy of telling not only owing to the

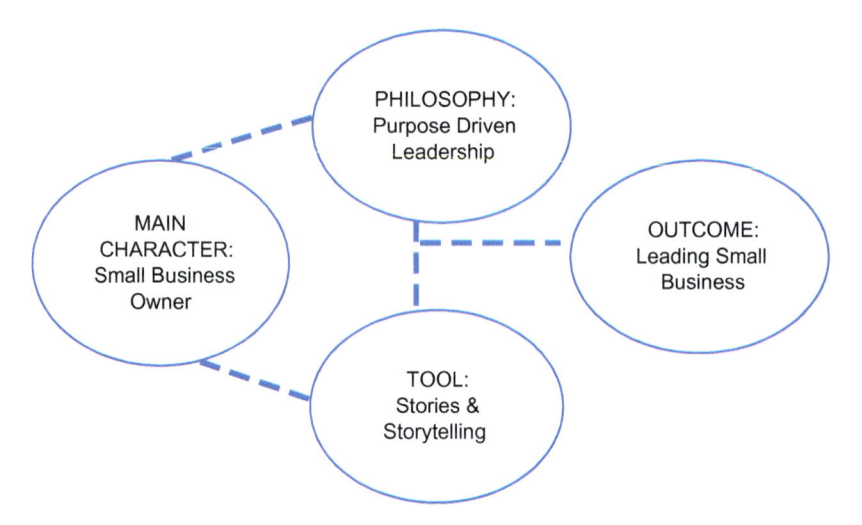

Fig. 9.1 Plot of the story—converging ideas. *Source* Authors own

population size and density of the small business sector, but because their leaders are the unsung heroes employing almost half of the UK's private sector workforce. Famous leaders of successful global businesses today such as Jeff Bezos, Amazon; Mary Barra, General Motors; Sir Richard Branson, Virgin Group, are regularly in the spotlight. The stories of these leaders are well known, well told, as manifest in the surplus of books, industry articles, and media attention testifying to their success. But, each company was once upon a time small and each leader started out with humble beginnings. This book recognised the need to grasp an understanding of the unique challenges, fears, and vulnerability experienced by leaders at the beginning of the journey and also in the first few critical years were the odds are stacked against them.

The plot signifies the convergence of three concepts; the small business owner as the main character, the philosophy of purpose driven leadership, and the power of stories and storytelling as a development and communication tool. Together these three concepts help to build a real story of leading small business (the outcome). The converging of ideas for the book is illustrated in Fig. 9.1.

The overall purpose of this book was to provoke interest in, and generate new knowledge of, effective small business leadership (i.e. the outcome) for the reader whether lecturer, student, practitioner, or small business entrepreneur. For the main character in the book—the small business owner, this can present a significant challenge. Most often, the practice and concept of leadership is considered irrelevant even though they are "doing" leadership everyday (Barnes et al. 2015). Given their unique approach to leading, in addition to the complexity, volatility, and ambiguity of the business world today, the purpose driven leadership philosophy was applied in the search of meaning. The research in the book provides evidence that this philosophy underpins the concept and endeavour of effective small business leadership with real business results. But, in order to find and tell leadership purpose effectively, the power of stories and storytelling in leadership development and communication was identified and justified as a critical tool for the leader. Moreover, the metaphorical expression and storytelling throughout the book invites the reader to participate in the plot of the story of leading small business.

9.2 Main Character—The Small Business Leader

There are many textbooks on the small business organisation and worthy of reading to understand the idiosyncrasies in structure and operation in comparison to larger more complex organisations. But, more recently it has been argued that the process of wealth creation for the small firm is in fact owner led (Bridge and O'Neill 2013). Notwithstanding the evidence of small business failure primarily attributed to a lack of leadership and management skills (CMI 2014), there is a greater need to understand the main character in order to make sense of the whole story. This required first defining the concept of leadership in the context of small business and second, understanding the practice of effective leadership. The research of this book points to the qualities of the entrepreneurial leader. Second, what sets effective small business owners apart is their practice of leadership. It is the ability to thrive in uncertainty, which requires an openness to new experiences, which entails a willingness to proceed in unpredictable environments and a drive and motivation at the edge of the unknown and the untried (Butler 2017).

To illustrate the practice of small business leadership and the impact upon the business performance and growth, the storytelling by eight entrepreneurial leaders operating in a wide range of sectors at various stages in the journey are told. Understanding the high failure rate of small businesses in the first five years, Chap. 7 tells the story of leading at the beginning of the journey. The stories from entrepreneurial leaders who have successfully navigated the challenges of business for more than ten years in Chap. 8 provide critical insight into the longer journey of leadership as well as the lessons learned along the way. These remarkable entrepreneurial leaders are stars not only of their own stories, but these small firms could be the big success stories of the future.

9.3 A Happy Ending?

This book has explored the concept and practice of effective small business leadership. Taking account the wider leadership experience of the author and the stories told herein, in addition to teaching and facilitating leadership development programmes, there are a number of home truths that demystify small business leadership. These factors underpin the key elements of success or 'happy endings' for the small business leader.

First of all, **leadership is not defined by CEO status**. Small business owners identify more easily with a title of manager or entrepreneur. But, to drive a business of any size or scale requires leadership. According to Brown (2015) a leader is anyone who holds her or himself accountable for finding potential in people or process, and it has nothing to do with position, status, and number of direct reports. Leadership as a title usually evokes the notion of followers in terms of staff, but even when there are no employees, the business owner or entrepreneur is required to lead investors, customers, suppliers, or processes. So regardless, if a new start-up business, a sole trader (with no employees) or a business with only a few employees, the success of the organisation commands strong leadership skills.

Second, **to lead is to learn**. Leadership develops daily, not in a day. Therefore, for small business owners seeking to grow, they must be able to learn and constantly. In doing so, small business leaders must understand what got them there won't keep them there. To avoid the danger of contentment with the status quo, small business owners must be self-aware and be teachable. In other words, be ready to learn from anyone, anywhere, and at anytime. Entrepreneurship requires the ability to handle and manage uncertainty on a daily basis (about what people think, accept or reject). In order to manage this type of vulnerability, small business owners must cultivate strong support networks and mentors to help shut out the noise, navigate the discomfort of courageous leadership, and find the resilience to drive the organisation towards its goals.

Thirdly, **effective leaders know their purpose.** The authenticity and genuine attributes in leading with purpose responds to the modern need of a new type of human psyche in leadership that encourages good people and innovation to survive and flourish (Denning 2005). But most of all, purpose driven leadership yields exceptional performance for the business, as well as promoting the greater mental well being and physical health of the leader (Craig and Snooks 2014). So, small business leaders should focus less on the external characteristics of leadership (traditionally viewed as extroverts, visionary motivators, hero types), but rather embrace the meaningful connection between who they are and what they do (Kiel 2015). For the small business leader it is easy to try and do everything, but less is more. It is more important for the leader to focus on a selected range of tasks relating to their leadership purpose that can be done well, and then delegate the rest to others.

Fourth, **storytelling is one of the most powerful weapons in leadership** (Gardner 1995). Stories are timeless, demographic proof, provide a form of recognition and engagement with people (employees, customers or investors), help deal with challenges and overcoming crisis, as well as an effective recruiting tool (Armstrong 1992). Stories have a sense making capability like no other leadership tool. Particularly in purpose driven leadership, stories are critical to finding, defining and telling purpose. The leaders of small firms should be passionate about their business, and stories can communicate emotion in a way that connects with employees and customers. But, effective leadership and storytelling relies on the ability of the leader to listen; the only way the leader can understand, build trust and earn respect. After all, the stories told by the small leader must be genuine, authentic, and relevant if to be endorsed and validated by followers of the business.

Finally, **kindness is good for business**. More and more people are accepting that kindness is good for business. For the small business leader connecting kindness to corporate is not only a pleasant way of doing business but it is also good for it. Kindness is confident and comes from the leader knowing there is enough room for everyone at the table. Controlled, negative, and belittling leadership is costly and ineffective for business creating a fragile culture that isolates staff and limits growth. Ultimately, giving or receiving kindness can warm, move, inspire, transform, quiet and calm like nothing else. The business world today could use more of all these things. So whether it is time, contacts, advice or resources, the leaders of small business should demonstrate that sharing is really caring; this type of abundance creates abundance.

References

Armstrong, David M. 1992. *Managing by storying around*. New York, NY: Doubleday.
Barnes, S., S. Kempster, and S. Smith. 2015. *LEADing small business: Business growth through leadership development*. Cheltenham: Edward Elgar.
Bridge, S., and K. O'Neill. 2013. *Understanding enterprise: Entrepreneurship and small business*, 4th ed. New York: Palgrave Macmillan.
Brown, B. 2015. *Daring greatly. How the courage to be vulnerable transforms the way we live, love, parent, and lead*. New York: Avery Publishing Group.
Butler, T. 2017. Hiring an entrepreneurial leader. *Harvard Business Review* 95 (2) March–April: 85–93.
CMI (Chartered Management Institute). 2014. Management 2020 report: Leadership to unlock long-term growth. *The commission on the future of leadership and management*.
Craig, N., and S. Snooks. 2014. From purpose to impact: Figure out your passion and put it to work. *Harvard Business Review* 92 (5): 105–111.
Denning, S. 2005. Transformational innovation. *Strategy and Leadership* 33 (3): 11–16.

Gardner, S. 1995. *Leading minds: An anatomy of leadership*. New York: Basic Books.

Kiel, F. 2015. *Return on character: The Real reason leaders and their companies win*. Boston, MA: Harvard Business Review Press.

Index

A

Action learning 92, 93, 101, 103, 105
Ambition 7, 23–25, 39, 40, 47, 106, 112, 136, 138, 143, 155, 161

B

Business life cycle 21–24, 43
Business owner 81, 100, 140, 141, 166

C

Communication 6, 12, 20, 66, 71, 74, 75, 81–83, 91, 119, 127, 147, 164, 165
Community of practice 93, 102, 105
Complexity 15, 60, 165
Confidence 23, 41, 55, 62, 78, 106, 116, 120, 127, 128, 138, 152, 161

E

Economic contribution 5, 14, 21
Effectiveness 26, 37, 70, 106, 158
Employees 5, 17–21, 23, 33, 40, 41, 43–45, 64, 65, 71, 72, 75–77, 81, 82, 90, 91, 93, 95, 96, 105–107, 115, 120, 121, 127, 128, 131, 137, 140, 143, 145, 152, 159, 166, 167

F

Failure 6, 7, 24, 34, 39, 40, 48, 62, 90, 100, 120, 125, 140, 165, 166
Federation of Small Business 16, 17, 24, 127

G

Government funding 24, 139, 141

I

Impact 2, 3, 8, 13, 14, 22, 23, 32, 33, 38, 39, 41–48, 55, 58, 62, 63, 66, 75, 78, 81, 93–96, 100, 103–107, 116, 117, 119, 127, 137, 138, 141, 155, 159, 160, 166

L

Leadership 2–8, 12, 24, 25, 27, 32–48, 53–64, 66, 72, 74–79, 84, 90–98, 100–107, 112, 113, 115, 119, 123, 126, 127, 132–134, 136–139, 141, 146, 156, 157, 161, 164–168

Lead2Grow 4, 7, 41, 46, 94–97, 99–107, 127, 130, 137, 138

Lessons learned 7, 70, 83, 92, 100–102, 136, 139, 143, 166

M

Marketing 4, 12, 15, 26, 42, 45, 71, 99, 100, 113, 119, 140, 153

Mentoring 43, 96, 98, 101–103, 105, 106, 137, 139, 147, 150

Metaphorical expression 3, 12, 13, 15, 74, 112, 136, 165

Micro firms 4, 7, 42, 45, 90, 91, 94, 95, 100–106, 138, 141

N

Narrative 3, 6, 15, 27, 72, 75, 76, 78–83, 91, 98, 163

Networks 15, 26, 43, 46, 95, 167

P

Performance 3, 6, 25, 26, 36, 39–41, 48, 59, 63, 82, 84, 90, 91, 94, 95, 98, 101, 104–107, 138, 140, 141, 157, 161, 166, 167

Plant life 5, 14, 15

Plot 7, 61, 97, 164, 165

Policy intervention 15, 24

Purpose 2–8, 32, 34, 35, 40, 41, 54–56, 58–66, 70, 73–82, 84, 95, 97, 98, 100, 101, 103–105, 112–114, 116, 117, 133, 134, 138, 141, 143, 144, 151, 152, 155, 158, 159, 164, 165, 167

R

Reflection 13, 15, 60, 65, 76, 79, 90–92, 97, 98, 101, 102, 115, 127

Relationships 2, 26, 56, 60, 79, 93, 121, 140

Resilience 2, 7, 55, 59, 78, 81, 114, 144, 146, 167

Resources 15, 19, 21, 24, 25, 40, 46, 64, 94, 132, 143, 153, 168

S

Self-awareness 5, 7, 55, 57, 60, 76, 95, 97, 105, 119

Small business 2–8, 12, 15–27, 32–35, 38–48, 54, 62, 64–66, 73, 74, 76–78, 81, 84, 90, 91, 93, 95, 105–107, 112, 134, 136, 138, 140–142, 161, 164–168

SME 18, 45

Social contribution 5, 14

Stories 2, 3, 6, 7, 14, 17, 54, 61, 64, 70–80, 82–84, 91, 97, 134, 136, 146, 161, 164–168
Storytelling 3, 5, 6, 70–74, 81–84, 101, 112, 164–168
Strategy 3, 12, 13, 19, 26, 35, 41, 42, 47, 59, 64, 65, 72, 74, 95, 96, 101, 103, 117, 131, 139, 141, 147, 150, 153, 158, 161
Support 4, 7, 15, 19, 21, 23–25, 32, 38, 40, 41, 43–48, 79, 80, 82, 92–96, 102, 107, 120, 121, 125, 126, 128–130, 136–141, 143, 146, 153, 158, 159, 167
Survival 2, 5, 16, 22, 25, 27, 40, 43, 46, 47, 62, 112, 138, 140, 141, 144, 146, 156, 157

U
UK Commission for Employment and Skills 46

V
Vulnerability 5, 56, 79, 82, 83, 96, 112, 117, 164, 167

CPI Antony Rowe
Chippenham, UK
2017-11-09 12:11